WITH

WIT

W9-ABZ-578

BULLOCK CARTS
AND MOTORBIKES
Ancient India on a New Road

BULLOCK CARTS

ANCIENT INDI

Illustrated with photographs by Sunil Janah

BETH ROY

AND MOTORBIKES

ON A NEW ROAD

ATHENEUM 1972 NEW YORK

All photographs are by Sunil Janah,
with the exception of the first photograph
in the first insert, which was taken by Robert Katz.

Contents

Introduction:
Bullock Carts, Motorbikes
and the Road They Travel

IN THE MIDDLE of the pitted one-lane road stood a sleepy Brahma bull. From afar came the roar of a speeding motorbike. The great, unmovable beast stared indifferently as the machine tore nearer and nearer. Without lessening its speed, the motorbike swerved and skidded around the bull, veering perilously close to the edge of the embanked road. For an instant the cycle's image was reflected in the water that flooded the newly planted rice fields. Then the reflection was gone as the bike skidded back onto the narrow strip of pavement.

Sighing tensely, the motorcycle rider squinted into the setting sun. A speck far ahead grew quickly into the lazy form of an old peasant swaying atop a two-wheeled wooden cart. The farmer's hand fondled the tail of one of the clumsy-looking long-horned bulls that pulled the cart. To the beat of a sleepy rhythm the hairy beasts plodded on and on; they might have had forever to cover the coming mile.

The motorcycle screeched up to the lumbering cart and

jerked to a dusty stop. The farmer pulled slightly on the tail in his hand. The bullocks halted, a change of pace that was very small.

"How far is it to the river?" called the young motorcyclist to the aged farmer.

The farmer's chin swayed doubtfully from side to side. His eyes scanned the glary horizon as if searching for the river hidden somewhere there.

"It's far," said the old man finally. "Sundown is only an hour or two away. Won't get to the river by then."

The motorcyclist frowned impatiently. "I hadn't thought it was so far away," he grumbled as he mounted his cycle and roared away.

The farmer stared after the dust of the fast-diminishing machine. He sucked his toothless gums, swung his chin another time or two and slowly twisted the bullock's tail, the signal to start again.

The bullocks heaved, stopped, pulled, stopped, strained and finally tugged the heavy cart into creaking, swaying slow motion. By the time the cart was moving steadily again, the motorcycle had reached the river.

The farmer seems to have made a mistake. Did he answer the motorcyclist's question without knowing the answer? No, for he had traveled the road many times. He knew it always took *him* more than two hours to reach the river from that spot. Of course, he had never traveled in anything speedier than his heavy old cart with its huge wooden wheels and slowly plodding bullocks. He had never stopped to consider that a faster-moving motorcycle would reach the river faster. Why should he trouble his mind with such theoretical problems when he would never travel on a motorcycle anyway?

As the motorcyclist stopped at the riverbank, he wiped his sweaty brow and cursed the old farmer for a fool. How *could* the old man not have known the river was so close? Why did he answer the question if he didn't know? It never occurred to the young man from the city that the farmer did know and had answered the question honestly.

Old and new, neither quite understanding the other: that's the tale of India. Of course, old and new live side by side everywhere in the world. A family is made up of parents and children. Cowboys today lasso their calves from horseback, then brand them with the latest electronic branding-instrument. Jumbo jets circle above the old palace of the English queen.

But in India the old is so much older, it survives so much more overwhelmingly, it is so much more isolated from what is new than in most other places.

The mud houses of India's villages are built in the same ways they were many thousands of years ago. Farmers follow bullocks pulling curved plows just as they did at the dawn of civilization. Rural folk still communicate with one another as people everywhere used to before there were telephones: they go visiting. At night millions of village women kindle flames for light. They draw water in buckets from ancient wells and scour their pots with ashes. Even religion, the Hinduism practiced by most people in India, is much the same today as it was six thousand years ago when the Indus Valley civilization flourished.

The Indus Valley civilization is the earliest yet discovered in India and one of the earliest known anywhere in the world. Indian cities were old five hundred years before the first cities are believed to have been built in China. These prehistoric urban communities of India, contemporaries of those in Mesopotamia from which western civilization grew, were impressively organized. The grandest structures were not the palaces and tombs of kings but the homes of citizens. Two-story houses were built of baked bricks. Elaborate bathrooms connected with efficient municipal drains. In these houses lived craftsmen and merchants, administrators and farmers, soldiers and priests. Crafts abounded, and cotton textiles were manufactured in plenty, although the western world would not develop the use of cotton for clothing for another three thousand years.

Western civilization is as old as that of India, but it is not nearly so continuous. Western antiquity is linked with the present through memories called history. Indian antiquity *is* the present; the present is history.

The great epics of each civilization illustrate the difference clearly. Every western schoolchild learns that the *Iliad* and the *Odyssey* were epic poems of ancient Greece that played an immense role in Greek culture and therefore in the foundation of the modern world. But what child today reads the *Iliad* and the *Odyssey* naturally, easily, without the prodding command of a teacher? The Greek epics are studied, rather, as literary survivals from a very distant age. The quaint fighting gods and goddesses, the pride and arrogance of the heroes, the mythological creatures that wait to snare errant humans, may strike a modern reader as interesting. But they are not characters and incidents we accept as literally true.

At about the time the *Iliad* and the *Odyssey* were composed, epic narratives were also being created in India. Called the *Mahabharata* and the *Ramayana*, they grew and took form slowly over the centuries. The *Mahabharata* relates the history of a great war in ancient India. In the *Ramayana* a princess, wife of a royal exile named Rama, is kidnapped by a demon. The epic tells the story of Rama's efforts to recapture her.

At a time when the poems of Homer were listened to, adored and believed implicitly by spellbound audiences in

Greece, similar groups in India listened in the same way to the *Ramayana* and the *Mahabharata* as they were recited by toothless old women. Today, everywhere in the land, people still know the Indian epics word for word. Today children still listen enchanted, as children have listened for centuries past, to tales that their elders spin from the magically endless flax of the same epics. Today those elders have still, more often than not, never learned to read the tales they tell; they learned them as children from their own grandmothers and great-aunts.

To western children, Achilles is a difficult person in an impossible school lesson. To Hindu children, the characters of the *Ramayana* are living heroes and playmates: Hanuman, the so-very-human monkey who crossed the seas in loyal service to Rama and discovered the hiding place of the princess Sita; Laksman, Rama's brother, who devoted his life to the service of the exiled prince; Sita, the perfection of womanhood, whose single folly, an overwhelming desire for a golden deer, made possible her abduction. The name of goodness and manliness is Rama; the name of evil is Ravana, the many-headed demon king who stole Sita. Yet even Rama is sometimes stubborn and proud, even Ravana becomes tragically human as he recognizes defeat in the corpses of his slain sons.

Rama and Sita, Hanuman and Laksman have been known and loved in exactly the same way for three thousand years. Where else in the world can a wide-eyed child learn at his grandmother's knee the same tale that was learned by a child in the same way, among the same rice fields, in the same type of mud house, thirty centuries before?

It is this continuity that makes the contrast between old and new in India so striking. While the shadows of a candle play on the enrapt features of that village child hearing how Hanuman rode the wind over the seas, at that very moment another child only a few miles away is watching television, seeing films of an astronaut riding a different kind of wind across the vast spaces to the moon. However close the two children may be in miles, the distance in time is staggering.

Most of the people of India are more likely to listen to the *Ramayana* than to see a man walking on the moon. Only one out of every five Indians lives in a city, and only one in many thousands of those can hope to watch television. But a few Indians live thoroughly modern lives and are as totally unaware of the timelessness of life in the villages that surround them as the villagers are ignorant of TV and spaceships.

The division between "modern city" and "old-fashioned village" is not an exact one. Villagers may spend their evenings listening to radios. Women in cities continue to wear the old-fashioned flowing costume called a *sari*, just as their sisters do in the country, just as their great-grandmothers did decades ago.

Nonetheless, more of the village is old, more of the city new.

The farmer carries his rice to market on his ancient bullock cart. The modern city man whizzes to his office on a motorcycle.

Motorbike and bullock cart: both are India, a nation of variety and uniformity, of grace and clumsiness, of beauty and misery, of riches and poverty, of old and new.

What is old is unlike anything a modern child of the West has ever known. Yet it is human, and therefore it is understandable. What is new is similar to what is new everywhere . . . and yet it is never quite the same.

1

Brick, Steel and Wires: City of Today

A MOTORCYCLIST coming to Delhi from the villages to the northeast enters the city when he crosses the River Jumna. Leaving serene farmland, he jolts over a rickety steel-frame bridge and finds himself in the midst of both modern bustle and medieval grandeur.

The motorcyclist turns off the bridge on Ring Road, a four-lane divided highway encircling the entire city. The speedway announces to the new arrival that Delhi is a modern metropolis. Yet it is also a place of history: red Moghul walls loom immediately into view on the right. And above the high stone fortress battlements rise the graceful arches of the palace of Red Fort. The motorcyclist drives fast, yet it takes some time for him to pass the long walls of the fort. When he does, he finds more walls on his right, these binding together the flat-topped houses of the old city. From some of those dilapidated roofs now rise television antennae.

Beyond the old walled city rise the smokestacks of factories and the towers of Delhi's electric power plant. The cyclist passes long modern government-buildings in a rainbow of styles, all the latest. He glances to the left to see the progress being made at the site of a new bridge over the river; more industry in Delhi has made for more traffic, and the old bridge is no longer adequate. A railway track passes near the construction site. As the cyclist bumps over the level crossing, he stares straight ahead. He does not want to look toward the slum city crowding against the track. Its tiny hovels are squeezed as closely together as piglets seeking mutual comfort in a hostile farmyard.

Now the motorcyclist turns right, away from the river. The fields through which he briefly passes are strikingly quiet after the clatter of Ring Road. The sense of deserted stillness is strengthened as the young man reaches the abandoned site of an international fair held many years ago. High above the grounds a rusting steel-frame globe overlooks the desolation.

These ruins of the twentieth century are a fit introduction to the walls that now suddenly loom into view. Built of massive boulders artfully fitted together to form its winding walls, another Moghul fortress, Purana Qila, or the Old Fort, was built by one of the earliest emperors. An ancient city called Indraprastha, thought by many modern scholars to be mythological, is said to have stood on the same site many, many centuries before the fortress was built. The modern city of Delhi has built an enormous zoo and a fashionable suburb at its base. The suburb is named Sundar Nagar, the Beautiful City, and the motorbike is now hurrying past it. Around the doorsteps of the three-story houses, all freshly painted in pastel colors, are small gardens lushly planted with leafy tropical trees and colorful flowers.

The serenity of Purana Qila and of the suburb does not, however, spill over into the road. It is a busy thoroughfare, crowded with every type of vehicle imaginable, plus a few that go well beyond the possibilities of fantasy. Taxis weave crazily in and out of slow-moving traffic to the left (cars here drive on the left side of the road, not the right). Bullock carts squeak along; the huge beasts seem oblivious to the chaos all around them—they move as if they were lolling along some village lane. Motorcycles brush the rumps of the bulls as they career past. Motor rickshaws buzz monotonously along their very unmonotonous way. Affectionately known as mosquitoes, these three-wheelers consist of the front half of a motor scooter fitted with a carriage for two behind. They can't go very fast, but they make up in tenacity what they lack in velocity. It is against a rickshaw-driver's principles to slow down or to stop. Confronted with a traffic jam or with a vehicle moving more slowly than his own, the rickshaw-*wallah* will pull out into the lane of oncoming traffic and ride casually through the opposition, who then add their indignant beeps to the general mayhem. The only road-creature for which the rickshaw-*wallah* may show some respect is the double-decker bus. In general, buses, with their clouds of exhaust and monstrously roaring engines, dominate the entire storm of traffic.

Our motorcyclist finally leaves the maelstrom, turning left onto a quieter street. He gracefully arches around one of Delhi's many traffic circles. In the middle of this one is a thousand-year-old mosque, or Muslim prayer-house. Some of the blue and green tiles that once covered its domed roof are still intact. Across the mosque falls the shadow of the Oberoi Intercontinental Hotel, a skyscraper full of luxury and modern conveniences.

Just past the traffic circle the motorcyclist turns off into his suburb. He rounds another circle and follows a road that runs beside a magnificent old wall, now in ruins. Inside is the tomb of the Emperor Humayun. The red stone domes and towers of Humayun's Tomb are everywhere visible from the upper stories of the neighborhood, a minor Taj Mahal in the very back yards of this middle-class suburb.

So familiar is the lovely tomb to the cyclist that he hardly glances at it as he turns into the driveway of his house. Inside a steel gate he parks his cycle, crosses a paved courtyard planted at the edges with roses and lilies, and enters the house.

In richer lands not very much can be guessed about a man from the simple fact that he owns a motorcycle. But in India, where poverty is the general rule, a man with a motorcycle is immediately known to be relatively wealthy. Today the roads of Delhi are full of roaring motorbikes at rush hour. An ordinary motorcyclist is apt to be a clerk working in a business office.

Only the wealthy own motorcycles in India; thousands of clerks ride them to work in Delhi: what seems to be a riddle is a clue to the land. An office clerk earning only a hundred dollars a month is well-off in India. Delhi, a city inhabited very largely by such people, is thus a rich city.

For the man with a family and an income of a hundred dollars a month, a motorcycle makes sense. A car would cost as much as he earns in almost three years. Gas and servicing would consume a fourth of his salary. Buses, on the other hand, would be cheap, but they are uninviting. Whether the day be a scorcher of a hundred and ten or a wintry one when the mercury drops to forty-five, whether it be a rainy monsoon morning or an afternoon when the summer wind whips up a dust storm that makes the eyes run and the throat burn: there is no time in Delhi when it is pleasant to stand for an hour waiting for a bus. Even when a bus finally comes, the driver is apt to halt a block from the bus stand, in the middle of heavy traffic. By the time the would-be passenger has run to it, dodging speeding traffic along the way, the bus will most probably be in motion again. Even if the man-who-might-have-had-a-motorcycle reaches the bus in time, it will probably be so crowded that he will gain nothing more than a toehold on the packed running-board and will travel to his office hanging perilously over the racing roadway.

Convenience is enough to sell a motorcycle. But convenience is not its only value. A motorbike represents victory to the man who owns one: victory over poverty, victory over the village, victory over much that is old-fashioned and traditional in his life; victory, in short, over the bullock cart.

The home of the man with a motorcycle also cries out that here is a person of today; sometimes, in fact, it cries out a little too loudly to be entirely believed. The house is built of brick, cemented over and painted white or buff or pink. In New Delhi it is probably two stories tall, with an extra room up on the flat roof. The windows are glass-paned, but they are hinged and swing like doors. Both windows and doors, which have no knobs, are shut with a small metal bolt. The floors are either plain cement or a highly polished poured-cement seeded with tiny chips of stone and glass. Called terrazzo elsewhere, this flooring is called mosaic in India, a reference, possibly, to the days when floors in elegant houses were made up of colorful tiles pieced together in intricate mosaic designs.

The front door of the house opens onto the "drawing-*cum*-dining room," a living room with a dining table at the far end. The furniture is made of wood, beautifully grained teak covered with a glossy varnish. Round tapered legs, plastic cane backs and seats on the chairs, plastic upholstery on the sofa, squat rectangular coffee-table, announce to the visitor that this is a modern home. India has been famed through the ages for its textiles; it is still the home of cottons and silks so fine that they are prized throughout the world. Yet up-to-date Indians value synthetics above all other materials. Muslins as soft as the wind and silks as sleek as the dew are commonplace. Nylon, plastic, Dacron—now *those* are things to sigh over and to covet!

An area rug stands before the sofa. A quick glance would suggest that it is one of the fine carpets so valued in other lands. But a closer look proves that its colors are less subtle, its pattern more crude, its weave far coarser than are those of its more famous counterparts. It is an inexpensive, commonly used type of carpet woven by hand in the small towns of India's great north-central plain.

It would be reasonable to expect the dining table with its six straight-backed chairs to be the focus of the dining area. It is not. That honor goes to the refrigerator, proudly placed on a wooden stand near the head of the table. The refrigerator, like the motorcycle, is an important symbol of the family's place in a complicated society, and a very prestigious place it is. How, then, can the refrigerator be hidden in a never-seen kitchen?

Over both sofa and dining table whirl big ceiling-fans. No room, office, veranda or shop is without them if they can be afforded. They are surprisingly effective. Even many of the very wealthy few who can afford air-conditioners (and who have them in their windows as proof that they can afford them) prefer to use the ceiling fans instead.

All around the drawing-*cum*-dining room are photographs and knickknacks. Shelves built into the walls, very fancy with swirling ends and carved supports, are showcases for the various objects of which the family is proud. Wooden birds, tiny vases, Swiss clocks, imported dolls, souvenirs from world fairs and almost anything else made outside India are thought worthy of display. Only rarely do the wood carvings, brass vases or other fine handicrafts of India, so prized elsewhere in the world, find places on the crowded showcases of well-to-do homes in New Delhi. Doilies decorate the furniture; embroidered cloths cover the end tables. Everything is well dusted and precisely in its place. Woe to the child who touches anything in the drawing-*cum*-dining room!

Fortunately, the rest of the house is considerably less formal. In fact, to pass from the drawing room to the back bedrooms of many homes is to journey from one age to another. Just behind the modern face of the house, traditional architecture reasserts itself in the form of a courtyard. This is ordinarily an unattractive concrete square, decorated with old buckets and rags, a *charpoy*, or rope bed, standing upright against one wall, a discarded bicycle rusting near another. The family is not, after all, so thoroughly liberated from the past of its land. Just as in the villages today, this courtyard, not the drawing room, is the center of family life. Nothing really happens in the urban courtyard, yet everything happens around it. To go to the bedrooms, the kitchen or the bathroom, to buy vegetables or fruits from the vendors who call their wares all day long, to hang wet laundry or dry damp lentils, access to the courtyard is necessary.

The kitchen, its screened door opening onto the courtyard, is a long room with a concrete counter running along one wall. The stove sits at the end of the counter. It is only a double gas-ring fed from a cylinder of butane, rather like a camp stove. Yet it represents a notable advance in the urban standard of living. Before these butane stoves became available in the 1960's, all cooking was done on coal, wood or cow-dung fires (and still is in the towns and villages). To be able to start a fire with a single match and the simple turn of a knob is an enormous advance. The convenience is only slightly marred by the necessity of replacing the cylinder when it runs out of gas, and the odd fact that it does seem to run out mostly on holidays, when the supply depot is closed.

Above the kitchen counter are concrete shelves, doorless and revealing the family's stock of cookware: round-bottomed frying pans, aluminum pots for boiling milk, long-handled brass or steel cooking spoons, tongs for handling hot handleless pots, a tombstonelike block for grinding spices, a slightly bowled circular iron griddle for cooking bread patties called *chapatis*. Everyday tumblers and plates are also usually stacked on these shelves. Good china is kept in a glass-doored cabinet in the dining room, where it may be admired and counted by visitors. Near the stove stand neat rows of jars, previously filled with jam, now containing the many spices used for cooking the pungent curries and lentils of India: red chili and yellow turmeric, white and black cardamom, brown cumin, plus a dozen other multicolored seeds and powders.

These spices supply the only brightness to a drab, rarely painted, ill-lighted kitchen. Everything here proclaims, This is a place for work; let the frills remain in the drawing-*cum*-dining room, where visitors may admire them. There is also a whisper about the kitchen that its drabness is in keeping with the place of cooks and womenfolk in a society where work is thought to be ignoble.

No brightly scoured white sink relieves the smudged dreariness. Instead, there is a heavy basin made of the same concrete as the floors and the counters. Since the material is porous, it retains moisture, and black mold grows in the corners. Housewives grumble over their constant battle with the mold, but the men who pay the bills usually regard porcelain basins as too expensive and would rather promise to replace the stone one in a few years than spend the money. A careless servant, they argue, might too easily drop an iron griddle into a shiny white sink and destroy what would be a valuable property.

Actually, the risk is largely imaginary. Most servants refuse to wash up in the basin anyway. Usually villagefolk by origin, cleaning girls are accustomed to working at floor level, for the villages have neither sinks nor running water. Ofter servants stipulate when taking a job that they must be permitted to wash the dishes from a tap below the basin, letting the water run over the floor and flow away, eventually, through a drain near the faucet.

Porcelain sinks are not, however, altogether banned. Outside the kitchen door there is one attached to the wall of the courtyard. Since people eat with their hands, everyone washes well, before and after every meal. The courtyard sink is for public hand-washing.

Across the courtyard are the bedrooms, usually two or three in a modern New Delhi home. Like the kitchen, their bareness contrasts sharply with the frills of the drawing room. Only a bed or two, a cabinet for keeping clothes, called an almirah, possibly a dressing table and the usual ceiling fan furnish the bedroom. The beds are flat boards on legs, covered with thin mattresses.

Many houses in New Delhi today have as many bathrooms as there are bedrooms. When there is more than one, there is usually a choice between "English style" and "Indian style." The latter offers a traditional type of toilet, sunk into the ground and sandwiched between two raised platforms the size and shape of a foot. Bathroom sinks are like the one in the courtyard. Showers consist simply of a shower head standing in a corner, with the floor below. In a land where the weather is usually so hot that everything dries in a moment, or so wet that nothing ever dries anyway, nobody worries about water on the bathroom floor. When one showers, so does the whole bathroom.

Another tiny room often stands at the very back of the

courtyard. Sometimes a servant's room, sometimes a store-room, sometimes a tiny family-temple, it guards the rear courtyard-door. This wide-opening double door opens onto an alley. Through it pass the servants. To it come the many vendors who cycle or walk Delhi's streets and alleyways from early morning until nightfall.

"*Sabji-wallah!*" calls the seller of vegetables. "Buy my potatoes, onions, tomatoes, eggplants." In a huge basket tied to the back of his bike he carries a magically complete stock of wares. Behind him comes the fruit seller, with his mangos and bananas and papayas and sweet-limes similarly carried. Others come with a particular item only—bananas or tomatoes or spinach—carried in a basket on their head. "*Mooooooochee!*" yells the shoemaker as he walks about with his lasts and stays slung over his shoulder. "*Kabari-wallah!*" shrills the man who buys old newspapers and tin cans. "*Jamen kalee kalee hain,*" sings the vendor of "black, black cherries." Almost anything can be bought from the courtyard door, almost any service availed of. Even carpets, carried on horse-drawn carts, can be purchased without ever leaving home.

The ground floor of the usual New Delhi affluent house is duplicated upstairs. Where the courtyard lies below, the flat above has a gallery onto which the doors open. Very often the houseowner lives with his family downstairs and rents out the upstairs apartment. On the roof, which is flat, an additional room or two are built. Sometimes these are used as servants' quarters, sometimes they are part of the second-story apartment, sometimes they are rented separately to another tenant. In any case, most of the roof remains, by city ordinance, an open terrace. Here people put out their *charpoys* and sleep during the hot nights of summer.

Such is the typical house of the typical man with a motorcycle. It is not, however, typical of city houses in India. It is very much the dwelling place of well-to-do people. And well-to-do people are a sad minority in this land of poverty. The houses of middle-class people, far greater in number, are far smaller, far less well furnished. Middle class, indeed privileged, by Indian standards, these city dwellers live well below the standards of some of America's poor. Their flats are tiny allotments in huge, monotonous buff-painted government projects or airless holes in dilapidated tenements. One or two minute rooms are all a family can hope for, whether that family consists of one or of fifteen people. Bathrooms and running water are usually shared by several families. The kitchen may be nothing more than the corner of a bedroom. Sitting rooms are unknown, for every bit of space is taken up by beds. The people who live in these dismal dwellings are civil servants, teachers, professors, young doctors. Their incomes are ten times higher than those of urban slum-dwellers.

On India's bottomless scale of poverty the slumfolk are at least as far below the tenement dwellers as the latter are below the families of men with automobiles. Makeshift huts, with walls of mud or straw or tin scraps, are the homes of the city poor. The lucky ones live packed into tiny rooms in brick buildings. In either case they live without sanitation or electricity. Dozens of families cluster around a single slow-running water tap or well. Cattle, dogs and flies demand their share of the scarce air, food and water. Imagine a sweltering night in June. The monsoon has begun, and rain is threatening to fall any moment. The temperature inside the one-room hut is one hundred and twenty. Twelve people lie in the twelve-foot-square space, on two beds. If you try to stand up, your head will hit the low ceiling. Mosquitoes have lined your arms and legs with itching bites. Bedbugs fill in the gaps. No fan stirs the foul air, for there is no electricity. If you want to splash cooling water on your face, you must tread over sleeping bodies in the pitch darkness, find your way outdoors, slosh through puddles and manure, and finally pump water from a well many yards from the house. So live the fortunate people who at least have a roof over their head.

On the pavements of every city, and in the empty lots of every town, live thousands more who haven't even a slum to call home. They may be more comfortable than the hovel livers on hot nights, but think of their wretchedness during the four months of constant rain or in the months of cold, when the Delhi newspapers report a few deaths each night from exposure.

For all the depths of urban poverty it reveals, New Delhi is, by Indian standards, a wealthy city. Fashionable suburbs are everywhere obvious. Colonies of clerks and factory workers lie on the far-distant outskirts of the city. Clusters of slums are cunningly hidden behind the impressively modern neighborhoods of the motorcycle owners. Old Delhi adjoins New Delhi; the two are in fact if not in law one metropolitan area. The old city also has a larger share of middle-class homes than have other places. But its buildings are aged and crowded together in narrow lanes. Around them run open drains. Colonies of monkeys inhabit their roofs. Here and there a charming garden or the stately ruin of an old wall adds moment to what might otherwise seem an ungainly, uninviting maze of dinginess.

Most other cities of India look far more like Old than like New Delhi. Actually, the standard of living in Calcutta or Bombay is, on the average, lower than that in the capital. Both places have their jet-sets and their families with great wealth, but such people are isolated exceptions. For the most part, the poor predominate. Even the well-to-do seem often to have been absorbed into the general poverty.

In Calcutta, for example, there stands one shabby box-shaped house among many. Its plaster is chipped, its shutters broken, its paint moldy. The stench of an open drain surrounding its base rises up to its barred windows. In this house live a prosperous factory-owner, his wife and baby daughter, their three servants and their chauffeur. The industrialist's cook lights a cow-dung and coal fire in a bucketlike stove identical to the one used in the straw slum-hovel inhabited by laborers across the road. The industrialist's bearer walks daily to a distant market to buy fresh food, for it has never occurred to the family to buy a refrigerator. The chair on which the rich industrialist sits while reading his morning paper is the same chair on which his grandfather sat fifty years before. Nobody remembers how long the cane bottom of that chair has needed reweaving.

The Calcutta factory-owner is no more stingy than he is unusual. When his wife dresses to attend a wedding, nobody could misjudge the wealth of her husband. She dons half-a-dozen gold necklaces, enormous jeweled earrings, exquisitely enameled bracelets, a ring on every finger and every toe. Why, then, doesn't her husband spend money on the things that most westerners, indeed most New Delhiites, would consider to be of first importance: refrigerator and gas stove, up-to-date furniture and a modern house? The answer is that the industrialist has never thought about buying such things. He lives in an atmosphere so thick with tradition and poverty that the value of modern possessions cannot penetrate. If his neighbors bought refrigerators, he would also. But his neighbors are shanty dwellers. His city is overwhelmingly poor, and so his own thinking is overwhelmed by that poverty.

The Calcutta industrialist drives to his factory in a motorcar, but his mind is of the cast of the bullock cart.

2

Portrait of Seema, Daughter of the City

THE BEAST called Typical in India is a slippery fish. No sooner do you identify something as Typical than it wriggles, eellike, out of your grip while a dozen contrary examples distract your attention. We have toured a "typical" city house in New Delhi and immediately seen how many other varieties of dwellings there are in urban India. We shall now meet a "typical" child of that "typical" house. Let the Calcutta industrialist be a reminder that other varieties of living styles abound.

Yet the life of the daughter of a New Delhi motorcycle-owner is important because it blends together so many different things. Traditional Indian ways, those that dictated the style of the industrialist in Calcutta, and the westernized manners of the Bombay jet-set combine under the flat roof of one well-to-do house in New Delhi. Together they emerge as something new, something Indian, yet something heartily familiar to a city child of the West.

Seema Gulati is a girl of twelve. Her parents, her older

brother, her baby sister Sujata, an old cook named Sunil and a nursemaid Krishna live with Seema in the ground floor apartment of a house just like the one we have explored. On the walls of the drawing-*cum*-dining room are photographs of Rita, Seema's older sister, who was married a few months ago and now lives in England with her doctor husband.

Seema's family is important to her, but her life does not center in her home. Her brother and sisters are either very much older or younger than she. Apart from eating and occupying the same quarters, she does things with her family only when there is a festival and parents and children join together in the rituals. Otherwise, Seema's interests are school and neighborhood play. She is outdoors with her friends whenever possible. She does not bring her friends home often, for her mother worries that they may disturb something in the drawing room, and her father complains of the noise.

Neither parent, on the other hand, really objects to Seema's being outdoors so much. They do not expect their children to help at home. The cook and the nursemaid, in fact, do so much of the work that even Mrs. Gulati has little to do. There is a bit of harping about homework, but the children have been trained to obedience early, and so there is little real conflict over it.

Indeed, Seema's home life is notable for its lack of open conflict, as well as for its lack of fun. When occasionally a source of friction between the generations does surface, it usually concerns a fairly minor matter. Clothing, for instance, caused many a small argument between Seema and her mother until recently. Seema was annoyed by her mother's insistence that she wear this or that clean, freshly pressed dress; the polished shoes, *not* the muddy ones; the green hairband in neatly combed hair. As a very small child, Seema had been pleased with pretty frocks. But as she grew older, she was irritated by her mother's overemphasis. Mrs. Gulati, Seema sensed, feared that the neighbors would judge the whole Gulati family by the mud on one child's shoes.

Not long ago, though, the squabbles ended, for Seema's interest in her appearance revived at the time of her sister's wedding. Weeks before the event the Gulatis' house was filled with elegant new saris. Visitors were regaled with showings of the new gold jewelry. Rita privately began trying to form her long black hair into a massive bun around an enormous rat. What color *bindi*, the decorative dot Indian women wear on their foreheads, should be used with which sari became a topic of great moment for the Gulati women. Seema was caught up in the feminine details. When the wedding was over and the excitement past, Seema's mother discovered with delight that she could no longer find fault with the appearance of her once stubborn daughter.

Even Seema's brother, nicknamed Lucky, noticed the change. From a college boy far more engrossed in his motor scooter and his beard than in his family, such recognition was notable.

For as long as Seema remembers, Lucky has regarded her as a subhuman pest who must be tolerated. With the new maturity proclaimed by her improved appearance has come a tiny element of friendship between the two. Now Lucky may deign to tell Seema that his new record is a popular hit from the latest movie (a fact of which Seema is generally already well aware), or to repeat to her a joke going the rounds of the campus. On the whole, though, Lucky and Seema remain strangers to each other.

Their father is hardly more intimate with Seema. To him, she is first and foremost a commodity to be disposed of on the marriage market. Of course, he assures himself and his wife, she is a superior commodity: bright, pretty, pert; he is proud of her.

Like every father with daughters, Mr. Gulati talks often of the marriages of his three girls. His relief that one marriage has been effected is only matched by his anxiety over the two still to come, although Seema's is about six years away and the baby is only nine months old. Mr. Gulati is very fond of telling acquaintances that he would never prevent a daughter of his from marrying a boy of her own choice, whatever his caste, religion or nationality might be. Very rarely does he add that he is fully confident none of them will make use of that privilege.

Rita did, in fact, ask her parents to arrange her marriage. She had had a childhood dream of becoming a doctor and living in England, a dream on which she knew her father frowned and which she never pursued in anything but fantasy. So Rita asked her father to find a doctor of their own caste who had settled in England. Dinesh was a perfect match: handsome, well established in London, son of a well-to-do Delhi family. His parents were even willing to take a lesser dowry from the Gulatis because their prospective daughter-in-law was beautiful. The papers were signed, the wedding jewelry purchased. Dinesh returned to India on a three-week holiday, married Rita and carried her off to London.

To Seema, her sister's story is the ultimate in romance. Sometimes, especially when she and her friends have just seen a Hollywood film, Seema spins dreams of romance that begin with love instead of with marriage. But when she talks it over with her friends later, they all agree, "Our fathers *must* choose for us. How can *we*, when we're so young and inexperienced?"

Seema is certain that her father will choose well. For years he has assured her frequently, "You're a lucky girl, Seema. I've saved a good dowry for you, and you'll have a good husband." Mr. Gulati is proud of his affluence. A well-paid engineer working for Indian Airlines, he came to Delhi in 1947 as a refugee from the new neighboring nation of Pakistan. Then he had nothing. With the help of preferred treatment by the Indian government, he has risen to the respected place of high-ranking executive and householder. Three years ago he built an upper story on his house. When his tenants, the family of a south Indian gentleman employed by the United States Information Service, moved in, Mr. Gulati added to his list of achievements the prestige of being a landlord.

Approving though society may be of Mr. Gulati, his daughter Seema finds him rather forbidding. It never occurs to her that she might talk freely with him, as she does with her mother. Mrs. Gulati looks like a girl of twenty. She is a slim, lively woman, proud of her escape from the flabby obesity that afflicts so many of her rich and idle neighbors. A college graduate with few interests outside her own doorway, Mrs. Gulati suffers from the boredom of her life. Sunil, the cook, manages the kitchen efficiently. Krishna, the nursemaid, relieves her of the involvements of motherhood. Another servant comes daily to clean the house. Mrs. Gulati spends much of her time haggling with the *sabji-wallah* who comes each morning with his load of vegetables on his bike. For hours she leans on her gate watching Seema play with her friends. Despite her boredom, though, she is satisfied with her marriage. All she might wish to make it perfect is a mother-in-law who knew how to whisper.

The older Gulatis live in the same part of the city, and Mrs. Gulati is often at her son's home. She is a woman trained to bellow: at the children, at the servants, at her daughter-in-law, even at chance visitors. So much in the habit of commanding is old Mrs. Gulati that she can no longer ask, muse nor whisper. She is a frightening lady to the small children of the neighborhood, but Seema is far less wary of her grandmother's noise than of her father's quiet authority.

Seema knows that the old woman's voice conceals a fierce warmth for her own family. Old Mrs. Gulati is proud of her only son; proud of her grandchildren; proud of her five married daughters, who live nearby and often visit; proud of her husband, a successful shopkeeper. In fact, Grandmother Gulati does not wholly believe that anything outside her own family truly exists.

Even her husband's battery shop is not entirely real to her, although it has provided her with a handsome home and five fine sons-in-law. To Grandfather Gulati, the shop is very real indeed. Like his son, he started in Delhi with nothing, and now he has a flourishing store in the very center of the city's business area. For years his business demanded most of his attention. Now he feels more free and is content to leave its daily running in the hands of assistants. Semiretirement suits him, for he has never been wholeheartedly a businessman. He is a homebody, more worried about his son and daughters and their families than about the state of the nation or of his store. He says little to anybody, but his smile is ready and warm and approving. He leaves the commands to his wife; she assumes that duty anyway. Both are happy, although in India it is more often the man who commands, the woman who obeys. And indeed, however loud Grandma may be, however mild Grandpa, the important decisions are still made by Mr. Gulati without any but the most formal advice from his wife.

Seema is fond of her grandfather, although only rarely is she able to show it. Custom dictates a formality between the children and Mr. Gulati. Each morning they greet him ritualistically, each night take his formal leave. Whatever restraint Seema feels in her grandfather's presence, however, flees when she is with Sunil, a man of about her grandfather's age. Sunil has cooked for the Gulatis for more years than Seema has been alive, since very shortly after her parents were married. In a village somewhere Sunil has a wife and children of his own. He sends them most of his wages and visits them once a year at Diwali, one of the major Hindu festivals. To the Gulati children, Sunil's journeys to the village are unreal. They, not his blood offspring, are his true children, Seema and the others feel. With a sigh, Sunil half agrees. He loves the Gulati children as warmly as they love him. He has watched them grow since their birth. His own children are always strangers, a year older than they were the visit before. By the time he becomes reacquainted with them, the week of his holiday is over.

Krishna, the *ayah*, or nursemaid, has worked for the Gulatis only since Sujata was born. Krishna is an illiterate girl from a distant province. She moved to Delhi six years ago with the employers she then had. Because her mother and sisters are so far away, Krishna has plunged herself into the life of the Gulatis. Warm and affectionate, sharp as rose thorns despite the fact that she cannot even write her own name, Krishna lost no time in becoming a true friend both to Seema's mother and to Seema. The baby regards Krishna as her mother; Mrs. Gulati is only a loving aunt, nice to play with but not to be depended on for important things. Krishna often tells the other *ayahs*, who gather to gossip in the park while their infant charges play, that her post would be ideal if only Grandmother Gulati lived a little farther away. To old Mrs. Gulati, Krishna is the symbol of the hostile Outside, to be kept in her place with an active and stinging tongue.

Krishna is not outsider enough to misjudge the power binding the Gulati family together. A more casual observer might see in the lack of visible affection a promise that the children, once grown, will drift away from their elders.

Krishna knows that Rita, thousands of miles away in a foreign land, is as close to her family in Delhi as if she lived next door. The Gulati family is conjugal; parents and children alone compose it. Yet it is a very small jump away from the joint family more common in India. Seema's father may not live with his parents, but he lives so near them that they might as well share one house. More often than not the elder Gulatis can be found at their son's house. More often than not they eat dinner there.

Indeed, it is at night around the dinner table that the true closeness of the Gulatis can be gauged. Having dispensed with the traditional joint family, the Gulatis have adopted the further innovation of dining together around one table. European style, the two Mrs. Gulatis set out plates, glasses of water and spoons on the table. When old Mr. Gulati's shop has closed at about eight, and the sound of his returning car is heard, Sunil quickly heats the food already cooked and spoons it into bowls to be set on the table. He then turns to the last-minute task of making *roti*. He has already mixed and kneaded a wet dough of whole-wheat flour and water. He now pulls off small balls of it, dips them in flour and rolls them out into flat disks. These he cooks briefly on the round iron griddle, turning them with his tough fingertips. When each one is slightly browned, he tosses it into the bare flames of the neighboring burner. Immediately, the disk puffs up like a blowfish. Sunil's fireproof fingers pull the finished *roti* out of the fire and drop it onto a plate. When three or four have been thus cooked, he delivers them hot to the dining table.

Roti, or their richer kinfolk *paratha* and *puri*, are the staples of the Punjabi diet. Elsewhere in India rice fills that role. The Gulatis eat *roti* twice a day, with rice an occasional side-dish.

Dal is also a regular item on the Gulati table. *Dal*, a lentil, grows in an astonishing number of varieties. It is boiled with turmeric, chili, ginger and coriander, and cooked until thick. To eat it, bits of *roti* are torn off and used as scoops. *Dal* can also be poured over rice as a kind of gravy.

The main dish on the Gulatis' dinner table is a curry made of vegetables, meat or eggs. *Sabji*, vegetables, is most common. Potatoes with cauliflower, carrots, spinach or any one of numerous other indigenous vegetables are fried with spices and lightly parboiled. The delectable dish that results is often unrecognizable for the vegetable it actually is. Okra, for instance, becomes, not a slimy mess, but a crisp and pungent delicacy. Everything is cooked with many spices, among which chili is prominent. Turmeric is always used as well, and people in this northwestern part of India are also fond of crushed ginger-root and fresh coriander leaves. Like *dal*, *sabji* is also scooped or pinched up with pulled-off bits of *roti*. In fact, most Indian food is eaten with the fingers. The only utensil placed on the table is a spoon, and it is used only for *dahi*, a yogurt dish that is as indispensable to a Punjabi meal as *roti* and *dal*. The yogurt is made daily at home, thinned with water, beaten, and mixed with boiled potatoes or diced onions, with fresh-cut chilies or little fried-cakes made from powdered *dal*, with carrots or any one of a dozen other ingredients. Then it is spiced with red chili powder and coriander, often artistically trailed on top to form a design. The taste, finally, bears as much resemblance to yogurt as the sari does to a miniskirt.

Meat and eggs often appear on the Gulati table, although many people in India are strict vegetarians. The meat is usually goat mutton, cubed and cooked in a spicy stew. The Gulatis, being modern, also eat chicken and pork; many Hindus do not, and no Hindu eats beef. But even when they eat meat, the eight people of Seema's family altogether consume less than two pounds. Think of an American longshoreman who consumes a pound of chopped meat all by himself in his two lunch hamburgers, and then goes home for a meat dinner. Meat forms the bulk of a western diet; for Indians, *dal* and vegetables, *roti* and rice are the substance, meat a mere incidental.

Many families in India eat no dessert, except on special occasions: a birthday or festival day. But old, pudgy Mrs. Gulati likes sweets, and so Sunil usually prepares a sweet dish made from milk in which rice or carrots have been boiled with sugar. Seema and Lucky also enjoy a frozen dessert called *kulfi*. Sunil boils sweetened milk until it thickens, then pours it into cone-shaped molds and puts them into the freezing compartment of the refrigerator. If nothing else has been prepared, Grandmother Gulati resorts to a traditional substitute: *gur*, a syrup made from the sap of date trees or from unrefined sugar. It, too, is scooped up on the handy *roti*.

What food Mrs. Gulati cannot buy from wandering salesmen, Sunil brings home from a nearby bazaar. It is one of hundreds of markets scattered all over the city, and it looks like thousands of other bazaars elsewhere in the towns and cities of India. From these markets food is carried home by servant, son or father. It is carried in the basket of a bicycle, in a car or on a motorcycle. Not more than a day before, these vegetables, meat and eggs were making another journey, from village to market on a bullock cart. The transit of food is one link between village and city. Sometimes it seems to be the only one, so vast are the differences between the two.

Outside the legislative assembly in Bangalore   ROBERT KATZ

New Delhi slum dwellers

Street corner in old Bhubaneswar, Onissa

Weaving in a "chauma" tribal bamboo hut in Tripina

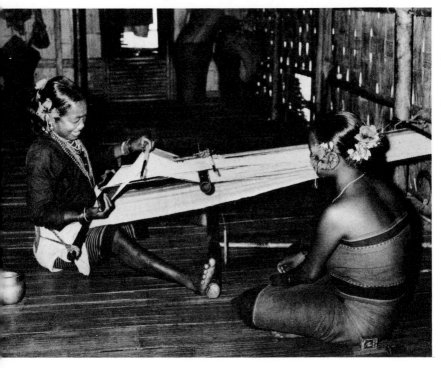

Girl in her kitchen in a worker's home, Bihar

A village in the Uttar Pradesh

Bathing water buffaloes, South India

Washing clothes in the Godivari River, Andhra, South India

Transplanting rice in a paddy field

Plowing rain-water-logged fields in West Bengal

Harvesting jute, West Bengal

Persia wheel used for irrigating wheat fields, Rajasthan

Watering paddy fields, South India

Fisherman throwing his net in a canal, West Bengal

Fishing in the Bay of Bengal

3

Clay, Straw and Moonlight:
Village of Always

WHEN THE whining roar of a motorcycle's engine coughs to a stop at the end of a day, its owner retires to a house of brick and glass. That is natural. Where else would the modern folk who drive motor vehicles live than in modern city homes?

When the stomp of bullocks' hooves is finally replaced at dusk by the chomping of straw in weary jaws, it is just as natural for the master of the beasts to leave his sandals at the doorway of a mud hut. For many centuries the ways of India's villagers have been as little changed as have been the habits of their patient, plodding, unrebellious bullocks. Now as then, their timeless path leads to dwellings built of clay, straw and moonlight.

Mud village houses can be sturdy structures, built without hurry or skimpiness. Walls are built up slowly, clay reinforced with straw piled thickly on top of hard-packed foundations, every few feet left to dry and harden under the tropical sun. Both mud and sun are plentiful, so much so in the case of the latter that the wise man uses plenty of the former when building his house. Well-constructed houses have thick walls, high ceilings, tiny wood-closed windows. There are no fans here, because there is no electricity to power them. So villagers retire to their huts, whenever duties in field or kitchen are not imperative, to sleep away the long broiling afternoons in the dark, protected coolness within.

Ceilings are beamed with huge bamboo poles built into the top edges of the walls. To these beams the roofing proper is attached. Usually it is a thick mat of straw woven so closely and expertly that it is entirely waterproof. To keep it this way, it is renewed every year or so. The thatching is a haven for birds, a ready-made source of nests perched on the bamboo beams. Despite the heavy protection the thick walls offer against the sun, the division between inside and outside is everywhere in the village a vague one. The feathered inhabitants of the ceilings fly freely about within the rooms, their flutter and chirp a cheerfully accepted part of the hut's charm. Wealthier villages boast red ceramic-tiled roofs or corrugated tins lashed to the bamboo poles. In these places the birds find the wherewithal for their nests outdoors but still build on the beams inside.

The floors are made of the same clay as the walls. Washed daily in large swirling motions, these floors are perfect play-surfaces for small children. Pounded, gouged, wet, scratched or drawn upon, mud floors are repaired in a minute with a swish of a damp cloth.

While mud and thatch are the most common building-materials in village India, the ways in which they are used vary considerably. Just as a green and white painted mansion in Maine and a rude log-cabin in Arkansas are both made from wood, so the many carefully groomed rooms clustering within the long clay wall of a landlord's domain and the wretched five-foot high peasant's one-room hut are both built of mud.

Bajitpur, a community of just over a thousand souls, is neither unusually rich nor hopelessly poor. Lying only three hundred miles north of the great city Calcutta, it is not far in distance from today's world of electricity, airplanes, running water and elevators. But the ways of Bajitpur are centuries removed from those of the city.

Through the village runs a rutted dirt lane, which winds its way a mile and a half from the nearest paved road, itself a single-laned travesty of a highway. So much a part of the fields and ponds among which it lies is the village, that one cannot tell exactly where it begins. Gradually, houses begin to cluster at the roadside, their doorsteps opening directly onto the dusty path. These clusters of houses grow in density. Between them an occasional vegetable patch or pond allows a view of the rich fields that stretch endlessly away over the flat countryside.

Just past a sharp bend in the road, at a place where it twists around a large pond shaded by the huge graceful leaves of banana trees and the tiny feathery ones of bending bamboos, there begins a house far larger than the others. The wall of the house, spotted here and there with a door, plays games with the lane, running straight toward it here, turning abruptly away there, stretching modestly parallel now and then. Its plan might have grown in the rich fantasy of a madman. Finally the road again turns sharply, and the end of the long wall comes into view.

Not one home but many are sheltered behind that wall. The house has grown into the unwieldy structure it now is over many years; the history of its additions and complexities is the history of the family living within. In the villages of India families are joint. Sons bring their wives home to their father's house and rear their children there, side by side with their brothers' children. When these boys—brothers and cousins—grow up, they in turn bring their wives into the joint household. Eventually, the family becomes immense, sprawling over three or four generations and including cousins two or three times removed. Then tensions arise, and one branch or another builds onto the house, removing itself to its new separate, yet attached, quarters. Thus has the house at Bajitpur grown.

The latest extension to the house is the one at the farthest end. Set back from the road about fifteen yards, with the wall of the parent quarters on one side and a placid pond on the other, it seems almost a separate, self-contained home. The front yard is serene and inviting. Along the neighboring wall is a rich vegetable-garden, full of tomatoes, cabbages, chili bushes and eggplants. A crisscross fence of bamboo reeds guards it from invasion by hungry cattle and goats. Opposite, running the length of the house, is the pond, shaded by an enormous tree bearing a small, juicy fruit called *lichu*.

Two doors are cut into the blank wall at the front of the house. The one nearest the pond is a small opening into an anteroom. The other is a wide, inviting double gateway into the main courtyard of the dwelling.

An unwitting visitor passing through the wide doorway might easily stumble against the doorstep, for it is an unremarkable mound of gray clay that divides the clay of outside from the clay of inside. To the right of the doorway is a cowshed. Four animals, munching the straw spread around a stored plow and an unused water pump, moo a comfortable welcome to the entering visitor.

Past the cows opens the busy majesty of the courtyard. Courtyards in New Delhi apartments are the geographic center of family life: everybody passes through them on their way elsewhere. In the village home the courtyard is not only a central passageway, it is the real focus of the activity of the household. Here fish is cut, lanterns cleaned and lighted at dusk, new tricycles mastered, grain weighed, clothing dried, babies bathed and sunned, neighbors fed on festival days, beds laid on very hot nights, small bladders relieved and local scandals announced. Here the seasons come to dwell: the scorching summer heat, which bakes the courtyard's clay into pale dust; the life-giving rains of the monsoon, which spawn pools of muddy water for children to play in; the brief cool winter, when flowers ring the square, turning the drab walls of the house into backgrounds for fairy festivals of color.

Three sides of the courtyard are framed by a veranda, a simple porch raised the height of a step or two, its roof a combination of thatch and corrugated tin. Every room but one (the anteroom, whose door is the small one in the front of the house) opens onto the veranda. Few rooms have access to others except by way of the veranda. The house is thus a square doughnut, with a hollow tube of rooms on the outside, the courtyard on the inside and the veranda in between.

The main wing of the house is the one in the rear. Its veranda, facing the cowshed and the entry doorway, is double the width of the other two arms of porch. Chairs and a bench are set here, for this porch serves as the true living room for the family. Two of the chairs are battered wooden straight-backed ones. The other two are reclining canvas beach-chairs, their once gay stripes now faded, immaculately clean and meticulously patched. At the other end of the veranda stands the only other furniture visible: an old, weathered cabinet, four shelves high. Once an elegant piece of furniture, its glass doors are now missing or broken, its finish long gone. Where once expensive crystal and patterned china might have rested proudly, now lie the toothbrushes, razors and broken toys of the village family. The cabinet has always been old, has always been there. Nobody remembers where it came from or a time when the family did not possess it.

Onto this veranda, between the chairs and the cabinet, open two doors, one to each of the two major rooms in the house. The left-hand one is the largest of all, a bedroom twenty-five feet long and fifteen feet wide. In a city house it would be the sitting room. But villagefolk have no space to spare for mere sitting; every room is a bedroom. For visitors there are always the chairs and the bench on the porch. Or they may sit, as the family does, on the bed inside.

This bed, called a *khat*, is more of a platform than a western-style bed. Simple planks of planed wood are pegged together and attached to stocky wooden legs at the four corners. The legs stand on bricks to discourage termites, who find little else to feed on in a mud house. During the night a thin mattress, first-cousin to a thick quilt, is unrolled from the head of the *khat*. A cotton spread is pulled over the mattress, a few small hard pillows are scattered about, and the bed is ready for use. When it is hot, people ordinarily don't cover themselves, although they sleep year round fully clothed in their daytime costumes. If the mosquitoes are biting or if the season is changing and the night air chilly, sleepers wrap themselves from head to toe in sheets, so that they look like stiff cocoons. Winter nights are very cold; people huddle cozily under heavy quilts called *lep*. Stuffed with cotton and covered with bright paisley fabric, a *lep* is as gay as it is warm.

On a single *khat* whole families sleep. Nobody has a fixed place. A child may sleep across the foot of the bed one night, curled around his father's head the next, stretched diagonally across the middle the third.

During the day, with the bedding rolled neatly to one side, the *khat* is used for sitting. People are accustomed to sitting cross-legged. Chairs are an ordeal to be borne on formal visits and at the movies. People complain bitterly of their stiff and aching muscles at the end of a film. Quickly they hurry home, slip off their shoes at the door, drop gracefully onto the *khat*, draw up their legs tailor-fashion and are comfortable.

Day and night, then, the *khat* is a useful piece of furniture. Indeed, most rooms contain nothing else. The large room of the house at Bajitpur is graced as well with a small table covered with a plastic cloth, two "good" straight-backed chairs and a wooden cabinet stenciled with the initials of the district school-board (one of the sons of the family was once president of the board). Another cupboard is built into the clay wall. Its wooden door is always padlocked, for it shelters from the foraging fingers of thieves and children the good crockery, brought out only for the most important company.

These few pieces of furniture are enough to mark the house with certainty as belonging to a well-to-do family. Only landlords in this part of India can boast such luxury as a plastic tablecloth, canvas beach-chairs and china valuable enough to be padlocked away.

Another sign of the status of the family is its possession of many photographs. The walls of the big room are covered with snapshots, neatly framed and glass-covered. Some of them are marriage photos, bride and groom stiffly scowling side by side. Others are death photos showing the garlanded faces of the laid-out corpses just before they were carried off to be cremated. Most, though, are snapshots of solemn-faced relatives, rigidly posing, eyes riveted on the camera's lens. The pictures are hung up high, their upper edges tilted out from the wall so that the faces of the two-dimensional people peer dolefully down at the flesh-and-blood folk beneath.

In addition to the symbols of wealth the room at Bajitpur contains the ordinary clutter of a village dwelling. Tin suitcases stand stacked against one wall. In them are stored silk saris, embroidered *kurtas*, lacy frocks: the family's holiday clothing. The one or two changes of costume that constitute everyday apparel hang from wooden pegs attached to the wall.

A smaller room next door to the big one and another long one upstairs, above the two, are similar in type if simpler in furnishing. The little one is filled with its *khat*, under which the tin suitcases are shoved. The upstairs room is long and low-ceilinged; its floor bounces slightly to the footfall. Instead of photographs, the walls of these rooms are decorated with calendars, some of them many years old, the dates overshadowed by large gory drawings of the fierce blue-black goddess Kali or of the demure mother-goddess Durga with a bloody man speared at her feet. Each of these rooms is assigned to one of the sons of the family and to his wife and children. The big room is used by the widowed grandmother or, more commonly, by the many visiting relatives who are always about.

At the end of the main veranda, just past the stairway to the upstairs room, is a modern addition to the house. When the sons of the household married and brought home their wives, they, being young men of advanced thought, decided to build a bathroom for their ladies. Until then, everyone had considered pond and fields to be all that was needed. What was built is precisely a bathroom: a room in which to bathe. A corrugated tin roof covers half the small space. The rest is open to the warming sunlight of winter. Big tin buckets hold water carried from the well. Old tin cans fitted with handles are mugs with which to scoop up water and pour. A hole in the floor leading to a ravine supplies the drainage system. Privacy, the great boon of the bathroom, is provided by a tin door just big enough to obscure the bather from neck to ankles.

The two bedrooms, the upstairs room and the prestigious bathroom compose the main line of the house. The rest of the dwelling is contained in the two wings that connect the outer wall with the main rooms, thus forming the square. On the left, nearest to the big room, is the kitchen. Long and narrow, it has a high ceiling and large windows, to make up for the lack of a chimney. A tin roof here would make cooking an intolerably hot job. Yet the thatched roof is a constant fire-hazard.

Fires are built twice daily in two "stoves" at the far end of the kitchen. The stoves are holes dug into the floor, their rims built up to form fluted cradles for round-bottomed pots. The arrangement of hole and cradle is simple and ingenious, craftily devised to minimize the drudgery of building coal or wood fires. Way across the vast empty space of the kitchen, at the end near the door, are crude wooden shelves. These are heavy with small bottles containing spices, with baskets of eggplants, potatoes, carrots, onions and cauliflowers, with old tins filled with sugar, flour, cereal, lentils, a clarified butter called *ghee*, syrups and mustard oil. Other foodstuffs more inviting to ants and flies are kept inside the only free-standing piece of furniture here: a small cabinet with sides of wire screen. In it are a pan of boiled milk, a bowl of leftover rice, a clay pot of sweets. The rest of the kitchen is open floor-space. Neighbors who have finished their cooking earlier sit against the walls on little boards, gossiping peacefully, their chatter punctuated by the sizzle of hot oil and the scrape of a large iron spoon on a rounded brass pot. Meals are served, as they are cooked, not on a table but on the kitchen floor, near the door.

Next to the kitchen is a small room with a double function.

Most obviously, it is a temple. Here *puja*, or worship, is performed. Tiny clay images of Hindu goddesses stand on a low table. Before them the women daily place blossoms, burning incense and offerings of fruit and sweets. The entire wall facing the altar is lined with shelves, filled to the breaking point with more tins, with jute sacks of rice and enormous caches of potatoes, with fruits in season, with stocks of home-ground spices and home-made oil.

Next to the temple-larder is a strange room. Small and containing the usual wooden *khat*, this room has beams stacked with discarded, mouse- and worm-eaten schoolbooks. It was once the schoolroom, when the sons of the family were young and the village had no school. Overshadowing all else, though, is a huge clay thing shaped like a beehive. It towers from floor to ceiling. At the top and the bottom of its bulge are small clay-sealed doors. It is a storage bin for rice and contains the family's emergency stock. Active supplies are kept elsewhere, but some is yearly deposited in the clay bin just in case rats or rain or thieves or visiting relatives should imperil the precious hoards of the household.

Leading off from the store-bedroom is the anteroom. Like every other room in the house, it doubles as a bedroom and contains the inevitable *khat*. Its function as a reception place is marked by a crude wooden bench along the only free wall. Here farmers, tax collectors, wandering vendors, resting wayfarers, all who are not important enough to be admitted to the inner courtyard, are allowed to be seated.

All that remains of the house proper is a large storeroom in the third wing, opposite the kitchen. Huge sacks of rice stand here, beside an enormous balancing-scale, its weights stacked in an impressive pyramid near the door.

Between the storeroom and the cowshed is a pathway. Under the overhang of the roof is stacked firewood. In its midst a stone statue leans casually against the cowshed wall. It is an eighteen-inch-high man, with an enormously fat belly and the head of an elephant: an image of Ganesh, one of the most popular Hindu gods. Ganesh, runs the legend, was fitted by his father with the elephant's head after a mishap—the details of which vary with the teller—in which he lost his own. A generation ago children playing in the fields dug up this statue. Nobody knows its age, and nobody cares; it was probably carved about five hundred years ago. The Ganesh statue is prized in Bajitpur because it represents a god. Had it represented a mortal, it would probably have been left to lie in a field for another five centuries.

Ganesh's pathway is a much frequented one, for it leads to a second courtyard, containing the well. This grassy, unkempt square of land separates the two neighboring households, which share the bounty of its old stone well. The system of drawing water is as ancient and simple as can be found anywhere in the world; it depends solely on brute woman-power, unaided by pulley or lever. In winter the aluminum buckets come up full to the brim, but in a hot summer after a poor monsoon there is scum more like mud than water in the pails.

The well is used only for drinking and cooking water. For anything else the family turns to the pond. To an outsider, the pond is strikingly beautiful, a symbol of all that village life is imagined to be. Still and shiny, its waters reflect the rich green of banana plants, the fullness of towering mango trees, the tall, slim curves of bamboo shoots. But to the people of the village, the calm beauty of the pond is no more notable than is the white porcelain finish of a bathtub to a city dweller. Dishwashing, bathing, scrubbing laundry, breeding fish, keeping ducks and swimming are the rightful uses of the pond. It is a simple possession like any other, the property of the landlord living beside it.

Even since the bathroom has been added to the house, almost everyone continues to bathe outdoors. Who wants to haul up all that water when he can step outside and immerse himself in cool brown waters? Indeed, most villagefolk feel not the least necessity of a bathroom, and most houses, even those of landlords, have none. People, often dozens at a time, bathe fully clothed in the nearest river or pond. Nobody desires privacy, for nobody finds the sight of another human being, his or her clothes clinging wetly to the body, at all remarkable or interesting.

Yet the folk of the house at Bajitpur did not rest content with a bathroom that nobody uses. They added as well an outhouse, and a brick one at that. The only structure in the village not built of mud, standing behind the house on the edge of the fields, which suffice for ordinary folks' needs, the outhouse is a self-conscious time-traveler from a far distant future. Its floor is wood; a hole opens in the center above a ravine. Whether his destination be outhouse or field, everyone carries with him a little brass pot of water. Every dawn sees a matter-of-fact procession of pot-carrying people.

Electricity is unknown in Bajitpur; many villagers have never seen its cutting glare. Darkness is a striking fact about the village, as physical a reality as the mud houses. Stars are not diamonds sparkling dimly in the heavens, but brilliant candle-flames. So near the earth do they seem that one would think a tall man reaching up on tiptoe might burn his finger-tips. When the moon is full, people greet each other with exclamations on how light it is. But even in pitch darkness their eyes know how to find unseeable glimmerings of light, and their feet never stumble. Walking in the dark is no idle exercise. Most households own a single kerosene lantern or two, and they are used indoors. If the family is not all gathered together, someone must go in darkness.

Indeed, the number of lanterns a family possesses is one of the symbols of its wealth. It is such slender distinctions that separate the existence of the village landlord from that of his tenant. The farmer has one lantern instead of three to pierce the same darkness, one bedroom instead of five built of the same mud, two beds instead of seven made of the same hard wood and covered with the same kind of thin fabric. The farmer has a rude bench like the landlord's on his veranda, but not a chair. His family eats from big brass platters just as the landlord does, but the farmer cannot offer a china plate to an important guest, if ever he entertains one.

The poorest farmers have no beds at all but huddle at night on rags spread on the floor. Without a single change of clothing, they squat meekly in courtyards of houses like the one in Bajitpur to beg old saris for their daughters who have grown too old to run naked. In winter they shiver together in corners, covered by a single thin cotton sheet. Nonetheless, that corner is made of the same stuff as is the courtyard in which they begged the sheet. Their house is small, its surface old and rutted by storms, its roof thin and leaky with time. But the substance of it is identical to that of the landlord's dwelling.

The well-off landlord dreams of a day when electricity and plumbing may come to his house; the poor farmer is not sure that such marvels really exist. Neither truly believes he will ever see such wizardry in his own village.

There are other villages, though, where the indoor toilet and the electric bulb have not only arrived but are taken for granted. Harischandrapur, for example, only sixty miles from Bajitpur, has paved roads, a railway station, electricity, telephones, a post office and even—crowning glory of modernization—a movie house.

To be sure, the hovels of farmers in Harischandrapur are like the very poorest mud huts in Bajitpur. But the landlords

sit on polished bedsteads under electric bulbs and feel themselves to be very citified indeed. No clay and thatch for them;
brick and concrete are the stuff of which they build their
houses. Their womenfolk cook on the same recessed stoves,
and water comes in aluminum pails. But they bathe indoors,
and their toilets are attached to their dwellings.

Four landlords with huge holdings, called *zamindars,* account for the prosperity of Harischandrapur's upper classes.
The *zamindars* live in sprawling mansions surrounded by
enormous gardens, but their incomes have recently been diminished by laws that limit the amount of land a man may
own. Today *zamindars* speak wistfully of the days of their real
wealth, when their fathers kept elephants, when elegant danc-
ing-girls performed in their music pavilions, when their stables
housed the finest breeds of stallions. Photographs on the walls
of their marble halls remind them of that past glory; relatives
stand solemnly before the Eiffel Tower in Paris or the Empire
State Building in New York. Nowadays the sons of those
travelers boast of the wealth of their fathers—and borrow
money from Bajitpur cousins, who once borrowed money from
them to study engineering abroad.

Relatively impoverished though they be, the *zamindars* are
still grand lords compared to the wretchedness of their tenants,
or even to the austerity that marks the lives of landlords in
Bajitpur. The *zamindars* have powerful connections: brothers
in Parliament, uncles who supply goods to the railways, cousins
who are bankers. They see to it that rural improvements spon-
sored by the government come first to Harischandrapur. They
have created of their village an oasis of advancement in a
desert of stagnation.

Other villages do sometimes receive the bounty of government programs. Usually they are communities that lie near
great cities like Delhi or along major highways. To these for-

tunate few, schools and hospitals, wells and electricity, are gradually being supplied. But the beneficiaries are not many. Other villages may have acquired a radio or a mud school in the last twenty years; they may have easier access to a hospital; there may be a telephone, which may even work sometimes, at the post office three miles away. But on the whole they have not yet had significant improvement in the essentials: housing, water supply, electricity, farming methods, clothing.

The major exception to the rule of stagnation is the Punjab, a wheat-growing area north of Delhi. Radios and bicycles are common in Punjabi villages. Tractors are rapidly replacing bullock-drawn plows. Simple farmers dream of sending their sons to America for postgraduate studies, while villagers in Bajitpur have never even heard of the United States. Peasants' houses in Punjab are built of brick and contain more furniture than a landlord's house in Bajitpur. About two-thirds of the Punjab's villages have electricity, although not every family can afford to use it.

India is a huge land. The distance from extreme north to south is two thousand miles, as far as from Boston to Dallas. To cross the country from east to west at its widest point, one must travel as far as from Los Angeles to St. Louis. All those miles contain an enormous diversity. Each region has its own language, its own style of dressing and of cooking, its distinctive dance and music, and its own way of building houses.

Throughout the northern-plains region, with the exception of Punjab, village houses differ only slightly from the ones in Bajitpur. Roofs may be tile instead of thatch, walls thinner, doors lower, rooms smaller, furniture more or less crude. But the basic construction and arrangement are the same.

Farther to the north and the south, however, the differences are more radical. The mighty Himalayas rim the northern edge of the Indian subcontinent. Trees, so scarce on the plains below, abound in the hills. Mountain homes are therefore often built of wood. Ramshackle affairs sprawling over the hillsides, their upper portions sometimes resemble Swiss chalets, while their bottoms are more like vertical shanties. Stone is also a common building-material in the mountains.

Cold dictates the accumulation of more furniture than is used on the plains. To sit barefoot on a mud floor when the temperature outdoors reaches one hundred and twenty is coolly practical. To do so when freezing gales bring the mercury down well below zero is impossible. Since wood is plentiful, chairs and tables are common at higher altitudes.

If weather compels the hill people to build solidly, it permits the folk of the balmy far south to live starkly near to nature. So warm and benign are the nights of the southern peninsula that straw shacks provide sufficient shelter. Walls are woven of split bamboo reeds, then lashed to bamboo poles rooted deep in the ground. Cyclones occasionally wreck most of the houses in an area. But if easily destroyed, the bamboo huts are also easily rebuilt. People are too poor to have many possessions. If they are not wearing all their clothing, they fold their "good" garments away in tin boxes, safe from wind and rain. Under such conditions there is good sense in building a very light house. A reed wall falling on one's head can't do as much damage as a clay wall can.

The walls of India's village homes tell tales of the lives of their inhabitants. The long house in Bajitpur spoke of the history of a joint family. The straw shacks of the south speak of a simple fatalism in the wake of ever-recurring disasters. Now we return to Bajitpur and learn more of the people who live there.

4

Portrait of Tinku, Boy of the Village

TINKU IS a boy of the village. Like most boys of Bajitpur, he is unaware of any life but the one he lives. He does not know that millions of other children in other Indian villages grow up eating foods slightly different from the ones he loves, learning songs with other lyrics, playing games with other names. Nor does he know that those millions of boys live in families very much like his own, in houses similar to his, in villages richer or poorer than Bajitpur but essentially the same. All Tinku knows is the life of his gigantic family, of his tiny village, of his household's cattle and pond and fields.

Tinku has one brother, two years older than he. But ask him how many children there are in his family, and he will reply, "We are six brothers and one sister." To Tinku, his cousins, offspring of his paternal uncles, are his own siblings. For his widowed grandmother and all her sons and their wives, including Tinku's parents, live together in a joint family.

In New Delhi, Seema lives with her parents, sister and brother only. Her grandparents, uncles, aunts, all live in their own separate homes. Seema's conjugal family is like families in America and in Europe. Increasingly, this kind of family is the rule of life in India's cities as well.

But the village people of India still cling to older customs. Land is held in common by the family; wages are pooled. The women cook together. Any woman may be called upon by any child for service. Toys belong to all the children; clothing and schoolbooks are passed from older to younger. To an outsider, the relationships in a family are baffling. The women are a distinct group, the children another, the men a third. Over them stand the elders. Which child was born of which mother? Which woman walked round the marriage fire seven times with which man? Mealtimes do nothing to sort out the units. The women as a team feed the children first, then the men, then help themselves. In Tinku's house, only when the individual families finally retire for the night into their separate rooms is it possible to know the relationships.

Above all the women is Tinku's grandmother. While her daughters-in-law toil in the kitchen throughout the day, she supervises from her special sanctuary, the temple and larder next door. When her sons sit in a semi-circle on the kitchen floor eating, she squats in the center directing the younger women to give this one more rice, that one the tail of the fish—which he adores—another a second helping of eggplant fritter. If Tinku skins his knee, he knows the fish his mother is frying will keep her from attending to him. Tinku goes instead to Grandmother for comfort and a turmeric poultice. More mundane services required by the younger children—a change of pants or a comforting few moments at the breast —are the business of Mother. But it is Grandmother who always has time to coax an unwilling child to drink a glass of milk, who can always be counted on to admire a newly captured butterfly.

When the women finish cooking at noontime, they bathe the children. Everyone tumbles into the pond under the eye of one of the ladies. Where swimming ends and bathing begins is difficult to say. When called to bathe, Tinku and his cousins may be unwilling to end the game they're playing. But once in the water, they have to be called often to come out. Tinku loves to clown. His bath consists of a frantic chase after quacking ducks, mock dismay at losing the bar of soap, comic cheers for his brother's attempt to swim the width of the pond and finally a strange functional deafness to his aunt's insistence that the bath is over and lunch is growing cold.

The other women have meanwhile been laying brass platters and brass tumblers on the veranda before the kitchen door. When the cheering children dash shivering from the pond and the chaotic screams of dressing fill the courtyard ("Those aren't my pants; they're someone else's!" "But yours aren't dry yet; you'll have to wear them." "Why can't I wear the new ones?" "They're put away in the suitcase. Wear your brother's instead."), rice is ladled onto the platters in great heaps. Fish curry is spooned over the rice, and water is poured from graceful brass urns into the tumblers. As the children finally come running to the veranda, sizzling-hot fried vegetables are placed on each platter.

Mealtime is punctuated by the demands of the children. "Aunt, isn't the *dal* ready yet? Give me some." "My rice is too hot! Mix it for me." "I want more *bhaja!*" The fried vegetables, so costly in oil absorbed and time spent cooking them, are a special delicacy to the children. As the boy's mother hesitates, Grandmother, who watches from her temple doorway, commands quietly, "Give it to him."

Each mother feeds her children the fish, a staple of the Bengali diet. Caught in rivers and ponds like the one beside Tinku's house, most varieties are sweet and fleshy, but chock full of tiny forked bones. The women mash bits of fish with their fingers, pick out the bones and pop small balls of the fillet into the open, birdlike mouths of their young.

The right hand is the only implement used for eating in the villages. Spoons and forks are exotic utensils; if Tinku and his cousins were suddenly expected to use them, they would rise hungry from their meal. Lack of practice aside, the rice, *roti, dal* and curries eaten in India lend themselves to finger-eating but are surprisingly elusive when tackled with utensils. Tinku's two-year-old cousin is already skilled at mixing his rice with curry or *dal,* forming it into small, compact balls and tossing them into his mouth with adept flicks of his thumb.

Without rice, or the *roti* that serves the same purpose in Punjab, it would be impossible to scoop up bare-handed the fluid curries and souplike *dal.* Rice is thus eaten twice daily if drought or flood has not made it so scarce that *roti* must grudgingly be resorted to for the evening meal. The quantities of rice consumed are enormous. Tinku alone can eat at a sitting a mound of rice that would fill the bellies of three western children his age. Many eat more bulk than westerners, but their diet is hardly an ideal one. Nutritious foods, particularly meat, eggs and fish, are far from abundant. Even on Seema's relatively well-stocked table the protein foods are small side-dishes. Indians are scandalized at the amount of meat and the paucity of rice westerners eat. Hearing tales of this topsy-turvy diet, Tinku's grandmother exclaims, "How hungry they must be! How do they fill their stomachs?"

With no forks and spoons, handwashing is a must both before and after meals. When they have finished their rice, drained their water tumblers, patted their stuffed bellies and belched, Tinku and his cousins make for the veranda near the stairway. There stands a plastic bucket of well water covered with a platter and capped with a tin mug. One of the mothers scoops water over the gluey hands of the youngsters, who stretch their arms over the veranda edge so that the water may pour into the flower bushes in the courtyard below.

Quiet play is all the heavy-bellied children can manage now. They sit chatting or matching stones under the big fruit tree outside while the women feed the men and then finish off the leftovers for their own meal.

All morning the heat has been growing from a dense threat into an oppressive solidity. By the time the midday meal is over, a fiery mass sits like a sleep-invoking devil on the villagers' chests. Even if they had not spent the morning in kitchens squatting over smoky stoves or standing in fields under the searing breath of the great sun or cycling to market amid choking swirls of dust from the lane, the heavy rice in their stomachs would be enough to send people yawning to bed. With petulant weariness the mothers coax their drowsy children indoors. Sleepy as they are, Tinku and the others resist feebly, briefly, before collapsing in heaps on the nearest *khat*.

Until the long dusk begins, the village is quiet. Farmers whose work demands a full day in the fields drowse in the scarce shade of trees. Cattle lie close to the cool dampness of mud walls. Ducks float quietly on still ponds. Late in the afternoon sari-draped women wander stealthily into the sleeping homes of neighbors for an hour of needlework and gossip. Otherwise, the village sleeps.

It awakes finally to teatime, a custom many believe to have been started by the British, who ruled India for two hundred years—until 1947. The king's rule may have changed the economy of India, but it altered the customs of his rural subjects surprisingly little. Twenty years after it had ended, Indians enjoyed a joke about two villagers who were informed that the government in Delhi had long been composed of

Indians. "I didn't know the British had left," commented one. Said the other, "I didn't know they had come!"

One of the very few customs that did stick, however, was that of afternoon tea. Many of India's people can afford no more than an occasional ceremonial cup, but rare is the man who does not yearn for tea daily. Tinku's family does drink it daily, when they awake in the morning and again after the long siesta. If there are visitors, cookies are brought from the market town two miles away. If the company is very important, sweets made from milk and sugar, *roshogolla* and *sandesh*, rich delicacies of which Bengalis are deservedly proud, are served as well.

As the family sits on the veranda sipping tea, the cool darkness of evening rolls mercifully into the courtyard. The women bring out lanterns to be cleaned and lighted. Slates and torn-leafed books are handed to the children for a brief spell of studying. After drilling the youngsters in the Bengali alphabet —*aw, ah, eeh, eee, kaw, khaw, gaw, ghaw*—the women vanish back into the kitchen. Another massive meal must be prepared.

Meanwhile, the men gather in the outer room to chat with visitors. Tenant farmers sit awkwardly on the wooden bench. Some ask in roundabout ways for supplies of seed or for decisions about allocations of land. Others bring a postcard received in the day's mail to be read by the landlord, for most of the villagers are illiterate. As Tinku's father and uncles finish their business, other neighbors arrive: a government officer, a tax collector, an agricultural-improvement instructor. These people come, not in their formal guises, but as friends, for the educated folk in the area are few and know each other well. Cousins also come from the other sections of the huge house, where live five related families of landlords. The men all have in common their interest in the crops and the weather, and their concern over rising prices and the latest events in the district's political arena. Conversation rarely strays far from these constant topics.

Now and then Tinku's father or one of his brothers calls out to the women: "Muni, bring a lantern." "Are you making tea?" "Give some matches!" The women slip in silently on bare feet, their eyes cast down, bearing lantern or tea or matchbox. Their heads are covered with the ends of their saris, their faces in shadow. Only the old woman may stay for a minute to listen, even to nod her covered head and add a word or two to the conversation. The younger women remain quiet.

The men sit in a closed circle on the wooden *khat*, the lantern in the center. Strange shadows are thrown on their faces by the flame. Cheekbones and brows are darkly accented; slight smiles or frowns are grotesquely magnified. Legs and backs are invisible.

On the other side of the pond, other groups of men are talking quietly in much the same manner. These are the farmers. They squat flat-footed against the sides of their huts, their thin faces lighted only by the glow of *biri*, tiny cigarlike cigarettes. Children play about their flanks, while their women prepare the evening meal in the courtyard within. The menu is less substantial than that of the landlords: less fish and meat, more *dal* and potato. But the curries are cooked in the same way. So also is the talk of the men the same: crops, weather, prices. The educated folk never drop in here; every member of this group tills the land by day. But in the morning the peasant children will join Tinku and his cousins in play. They know the same games, play them with the same verve. If Tinku is usually the one to decide which game it is to be, that is because his sparkle and intelligence make him a natural leader. Only lightly does the fact hang over these children that a peasant's son is rarely acknowledged to have the makings of a leader.

Whether their father's hands are calloused from the plow or soft with the privilege of the educated, the children all tire at about the same time. As their eyelids grow heavy, they gravitate toward the men's talk. In the glow of the lantern they drowse. With prods and gentle pushes from the men they finally heave themselves up and, yawning, shuffle toward the kitchen to demand food. Cooking is still going on, for the adults won't eat until nine or ten o'clock. But whatever is finished is served to the youngsters. Quickly they hand the food to their mouth; rhythmically they chew and swallow. Any child who has already fallen soundly asleep is laid across his mother' lap and fed, peacefully sleeping, his full portion of rice, curry and fish. Rarely do village children quarrel among themselves, but when they do, it is during the evening meal. As soon as they have cleared their platters and rinsed their hands, they crawl into a womanly lap or curl up just beyond the circle of light from the men's lantern. As the musical lilt of gossip in kitchen or anteroom beats warmly around their ears, they slip quietly into slumber. No one has said, "Go to sleep!" No one has ordered them into the exile of an isolated bedroom. Children sleep when they are sleepy, wherever they happen to be. The last duty at night of the mothers is to collect the slumbering children and deposit them in their beds.

Tinku's quiet evening intrusions into the life of his father are treasured by him. At other times he hardly sees the older man. Like Seema's, his contacts with the adult world are mostly with women. Because his mother spends so much time in the kitchen, and because she is expected to serve her husband and her mother-in-law before her children, Tinku is not so dependent on her as Seema is on Mrs. Gulati. Grandmother or aunt can usually tend to Tinku's needs just as well as mother. Yet Tinku's demands on whoever meets them are more insistent than any of Seema's. If Seema's mother answers, "A little later; I'm busy at the moment," Seema waits. But Tinku always wants to eat *now*, to wear *that* shirt and no other.

Tinku is more spirited in pressing his interests for two reasons. A boy is generally given more attention from birth than is a girl, so that he grows up believing his needs to be important. Moreover, the joint family leaves young children free from rules and commands, while hastening to meet their demands promptly. Whenever a baby cries, night or day, he is fed. Whenever nature calls, it is answered on the spot, without the impediment of diapers. No adult objects to mopping up after a small child.

Nor is any great burden of work fastened on young villagers' shoulders. Landlords' boys have no chores at all. Sons of farmers must help at the busiest seasons, such as the harvest. Other times their tasks are light: to take the cattle to water in the morning, riding lazily along on a big buffalo's back; to bring them home again at night; to fetch an occasional bucket of water for the women. Girls of whatever station may be asked to look after younger children. But the babies do not interfere very seriously with a little girl's play. An infant sits easily on the hip of an older child, even though the nursemaid may be only a little bit bigger than the baby she totes. The big sister who seems so heavily burdened is actually as nimble as her unladened brother, as quick at follow-the-leader, as agile at tag. If the game requires more motion still, the baby can always be plunked down in the dust and given a stone to gurgle over happily until the sister's turn at hopscotch or jumping rope is finished. More tricky aid—a change of clothes, a drink of milk—is the task of the older women.

If work weighs only lightly on these children, no heavier is the burden of school. If they go to school at all, the classroom takes up only an hour or two in the morning. After that the students are free to wander slowly home, where their slates are left on a shelf or under a *khat* until the next day. Only rarely does an adult remember that homework may be pending.

Into this serene childhood utopia a sudden evil wind blows when the youngster turns nine or ten. Then comes the thunderous question of marriage for a girl, of work for a boy. Now, Tinku is permitted to wrestle with his girl cousins; to bathe with them in the pond; to climb from their shoulders into a laden mango tree; to pull their braids as they struggle with their first piece of knitting; to listen breathlessly, leaning on their laps, as they recount the plot of a film seen in a distant market town. At ten, Tinku will be expected to address those same cousins with a distant restraint; to refrain at all costs from touching them, even accidentally; never to speak with them alone; never to show an undue interest in their handicrafts or gossip. The girls, at the same time, will be expected to keep their eyes lowered in the presence of Tinku, their former playmate; to giggle demurely when jesting with him, but never to show toward him a spirit as bold as they did when children. Those girl playmates will be busy with interviews by prospective in-laws. They will be practicing secretly to wear their first saris. They will be dreaming nightly of wedding jewelry and waking cold with sweat from nightmares about banishment to the home of a fierce father-in-law.

Boys of ten still dream of ripe mangos rather than of weddings, of cool ponds rather than of wives. They will not be married for another ten or fifteen years. But the marriageability of their female playmates affects them, too. At this time of sexual awakening, boys and girls in more modern lands begin to form new relationships with one another, to experiment and test and learn. But the boy of an Indian village finds himself alone in a girl-bereft world. All his female friends may not yet be married, but those who are not have shed the gay openness of girlhood and donned in its stead the shy, withdrawn manner of young Indian women. To a boy, a girl is an infant playmate or a spouse; she can be nothing else.

If marriage is not the immediate concern of an adolescent boy, work is. A village boy rarely wonders what he will do when he grows up. He knows. If his father is a farmer, he will be a farmer. If his father is a landlord, he will inherit land. If he has many brothers older than he, he may also become a teacher or a doctor or a government officer, but the decision is in the laps of his elders. When he reaches puberty, his grooming for work begins. He goes with his father to the fields. He is sent to a distant boarding-school. He is schooled in the intricacies of his family's landholdings and tenantry.

In recent years doubt, questioning and ultimately change have more and more often been infecting the obedience of middle-class rural youths. Very rarely do a boy's rebel spirits grow to the point of defiance so long as his father lives. But when the older man is gone, conflict begins. More and more often, brothers chafe in the close contact of the joint family. They bicker, weep and finally separate. Each conjugal family then goes its own way. For the younger brothers that way often leads to towns and cities. In the shadow of the ancestral home, in the grip of the authority of age, young men cannot feel in full control of their own lives. The impersonality of the metropolis offers a new life, frightening in many ways, yet hopeful, alive, free.

These young men, moving with their wives and children to new places and modern lives, represent another pace along India's road to a new age. It is a painfully hard step, and it is taken very, very slowly.

stop. Third-class compartments are crowded and chaotic; it is not hard to avoid the ticket collector. Big signs in the railway stations proclaim: "Ticketless travel is a social evil!" Since most ticketless travelers can't read and wouldn't know what a social evil was if they could, the signs do nothing to discourage the practice. The Madras study showed that three-fourths of the beggars in the city who had come by train from the surrounding villages had never bought a ticket.

Arriving in Madras, the young man was baffled. Never had he seen such traffic; it literally barred his way out of the big station. Never had he seen as many streets as were already visible from the spot in which he stood. In a village it is easy for a stranger to ask the first person he meets, "Where is the temple? Can I find food and shelter there?" But in the city, with so many people hurrying by, the young man could not be sure anyone would answer.

So he began hiking at random, his wife and children trailing after him. All were dusty, weary, their heads laden with bundles, their bellies empty. Unless they were lucky enough to happen upon a temple, they hiked until nightfall. Then, wherever they were, they came upon people making their bed on the pavement. Wearily the travelers lowered their bundles, rolled out their rags on the ground, listened anxiously to warnings from the old-timers to tie the covers to their toes lest they be stolen in the night, and clumsily obeyed. Finally they fell into a restless sleep. They had joined the ranks of the urban homeless.

Next day the young man went out with the others in search of work. If the gods smiled, he found a job as a laborer. Thereafter, occasional manual work kept him and his family in food, until the morning he woke up with the fever and runs that come to all who drink whatever impure water they can find. For days, for weeks, the fever continued; his wife and children begged for coins. A new family of beggars could be added to the statistics.

Often the migrants come to beggary by a shorter route, for they bring their illnesses full-blown with them from the village. It is often those very illnesses that start them on their journey. There is a superstitious faith in the villages that anything can be cured in the big city if only one is brave enough to go there. Once arrived, though, these people find the hospitals confusing and overcrowded, their staffs indifferent, their medicines adulterated. The path to beggary for the sick is steep and slippery.

Family quarrels, too, sometimes give the initial shove. When close-knit joint families fall apart, the event is so soul-shaking that people often quit their homes and villages and go in search of new lives.

Many of the beggarfolk were once shopkeepers, craftsmen, washermen, farmers. Of the women beggars in the Madras study, most were married and lived on the streets or in slums with their husbands and children. Half of the Madras beggars had lived by begging for at least five years at the time of the study. Only very rarely, though, were they the children of beggars.

For people like Gopal and his family in Calcutta, however, the prospects that begging will pass from one generation to the next as a way of life are very real. Gopal's grandparents and parents left their village, far to the east of the city, shortly after India became independent in 1947. With independence came the division of India and the establishment of the new Muslim nation, Pakistan. Gopal's people were Hindus, but they found their village on the Muslim side of the international border. The division was accompanied by a storm of religious slaughter. Horror-struck by the butchery all around them, certain that they too would eventually be victims, Gopal's grandparents and their children packed up their bundles in panic, left the ancestral village where their family had been cozily embedded for centuries, and joined a river of millions on their way blindly westward toward India. Along the way they passed millions going the other way, Muslims fleeing Hindu persecution in India.

The journey was filled with disease, hunger and attack from Muslim Pakistanis. All there was to cheer these homeless folk on their desperate way was the belief that they would be heartily welcomed by the land toward which they trekked. They expected to find there new lands, new houses, new and wealthier lives.

What they found instead was a Calcutta whose pavements were inhabited by millions of their kind, all fleeing the horrors of massacre at home. Sleeping space on the sidewalks was at a premium. At night the bodies of sleepers lay arm to arm, foot to foot, a solid human carpet of wretchedness. Thousands camped in the railroad stations, under bridges, in the arcades of bazaars. Gopal's grandfather, grandmother, father, uncle and aunt set up their cooking pots in a damp corner under the steel rafters of a mighty bridge spanning the Hooghly River.

When, months later, the stream of refugees slowed to a trickle, the government of India opened up new lands a hundred miles away and offered them to the homeless. Gopal's family was among those who went to begin life anew. Gopal's family was also among the many who quickly came back to the streets of Calcutta.

"It was not like home," Gopal's grandfather complained many years later. "We are used to lakes and rivers and lots of fish. There we had no rivers, no lakes, no fish. The land we tilled at home was mellow with the tilling of generations. This new land was full of stones. Never had it known the plow before.

"Yes, we had a house. We were helped to build it as soon

as we got there, and we built a good house of three rooms and a *puja* room and a kitchen hut." Gopal's grandfather shrugged his shoulders. "But it was not Bengal. That house could never have been our home."

The open skies and hard concrete sidewalks of Calcutta were Bengal; they could and did become home. Gopal's grandfather married his daughter and sons and saw them raise huge families on those same streets. Only after Gopal's birth, when the family already numbered twelve, did they obtain a single room in an abandoned barracks that had been built by the Americans during World War II.

Why did millions of Bengali refugees choose the streets rather than life in a new land? Uprooted from a way of life centuries old, they must have felt a sense of unreality wherever they went. Bengal was the one remaining link with the life that had been theirs before; and so they chose the streets.

Refugees across the country in Delhi were behaving quite differently. A similar influx had swamped the Indian capital, for Punjab, the bordering state, was divided between Pakistan and India just as Bengal had been. But the Punjabi refugees settled in new suburbs and townships. One of the latter, Faridabad, is today a flourishing industrial satellite to Delhi. Another refugee city, Chandigarh, was built by the famous French architect Le Corbusier and is one of the world's most modern planned cities.

It is difficult today to find on the streets of Delhi a refugee from the time of partition. Yet Delhi's pavements are nonetheless crowded with roofless folk. Like Madras, like every city in India, Delhi is a magnet for discontented villagers who believe government reports of great opportunities in town. So long as times are hard in the country, the great pools of the homeless and the beggars will never be drained from the cities' gutters.

The problem is monumental. Imagine that some disaster wiped out every dwelling in Washington, D. C., then moved on to Chicago, where it reduced all the homes to miserable collections of straw and waste tin. Conditions in these two cities would be about what they are for the poor in Calcutta today: almost a million souls homeless, more than three million living in slum huts. And every city of India suffers from similar, though slightly less extensive, conditions.

It is easy to assume that people take to beggary through a distaste for work. That mere laziness is too facile an explanation, though, is proved by the lack of reward it commands. Most beggars in Madras in 1956 earned about two dollars a month. Nine out of ten of them could afford to spend nothing on clothing; forty-nine out of fifty spent nothing on shelter. In other words, whatever pittance they received went solely for food.

Modern folk in places like Seema's New Delhi neighborhood are often angered by the fact that people give even those two meager dollars a month. To give, they say, encourages the bad habit of begging. When the tiny amount each beggar receives is multiplied by the enormous number of beggars in India, it amounts to a sizable fortune. Yet India is a land of poverty. Donors of alms are often very little richer than the beggars to whom they give. A coin dropped in a beggar's bowl may mean less food for the giver's family that day. The rich are rarely willing to sacrifice anything important for the benefit of a ragged beggar. The poor do so daily.

Why? Part of the reason is obvious. The man who is himself poor is apt to have more sympathy for one who begs. With no very large leap of his imagination the bony laborer can see himself standing ragged by the side of the road wailing for *baksheesh*, alms. Yet that explanation, while logical, does not go far enough. Most people are apt to feel sympathetic but passive. "I'm sorry for that man," they think, "but I can't give him anything without suffering myself. So, of course, I'll not give."

What supplies an added push toward generosity is religion. Begging is not simply tolerated by Hinduism, it is positively obligatory for certain people: religious students, holy men and elderly pilgrims. For others, there are times and conditions when begging is permissible. If a man's parents, wife or children are in need, he may beg on their behalf. If a person is without food for three days, he may beg, but he must consume what he is given on the same day, saving nothing for the morrow.

If begging is sometimes a Hindu rule, giving is always the law. Through charity one gains virtue. "The beggar who comes to the door of a householder," says a Hindu scripture, "is God disguised; to refuse him alms is to sin." That injunction is obeyed by most Hindus, especially by the poorer folk, who live closest to the strict letter of their creed. A beggar is rarely passed in the street or turned from a door without a coin, a handful of rice or a cold *roti*.

Still, to give is not necessarily to respect the one who receives. Begging is not a disgrace, but it does consign the beggar—unless he is a holy man—to a lowly position in Hindu society. He is left squatting in the dust outside the door, and his food is dropped from a height into his brass beggar's bowl.

But in India lack of respect does not imply lack of dignity. Beggars accept their role as mendicants and yet keep their self-respect. On hot days one shriveled-up white-bearded man in New Delhi will only beg from wealthy homes. Given a glass of tap water, he spills it on the ground and asks politely for "machine-*wallah pani*," cold water from the refrigerator "machine." If he is fed bread one day, he will not ask the next for food but for a rupee so that he may buy the *roti* he prefers.

However approving may be the attitude of Hinduism to begging, however casual its approach toward the want that breeds it, poverty is nonetheless ugly. Nowhere is its vileness more blatant than in Rishikesh, a sacred town in the Himalayas. Hundreds of pilgrims visiting the town walk along a pathway toward a hanging bridge over the holy River Ganges, which rushes down from its nearby source. Along that path sit lepers. Uniformly clothed in rags gray with age and use, they form a neat line, squatting at even intervals. Young women with babies, graybeards, men in their prime, all reach out hands with stumps of fingers and demand coins. Some expose raw wounds. Others bind their sores with cloths conspicuously smeared with blood. The sun grows hot, and the beggars prop up umbrellas to shade themselves, or construct ingenious structures of bamboo roofed with stretched cloth. The effect is that of a close-packed series of cages. At one end of the line a man sits making change for rupees, at a nominal charge. He gives the scene an appearance of normalcy, which is reinforced by the cheerful chatting of the beggars in the intervals between pilgrims. They nod approvingly to each other at the generosity of some donor; they giggle at the oddness of a hippie's costume; they vent righteous anger at the miserliness of some young Indian sightseers. But as soon as a new pilgrim comes into sight, the tone changes quickly to piteous wails that, multiplied as they are by hundreds, seem literally to shake the mountains. And the pilgrims march past, admiring the scenery, exclaiming pleasantly at first view of the hanging bridge, exchanging cheerful comments on their journey, and now and then tossing a coin casually to the nearest leper.

A Hindu might find the scene at Rishikesh natural and acceptable. But to a non-Hindu, the avenue of lepers and the stream of unmoved pilgrims flowing past them are deeply shocking. Rishikesh suggests an acceptance of suffering and poverty so profound that it can only imply an inability of one human being to see another as human.

Yet it is not fair to blame Hinduism for this callousness. That would be to confuse cause and effect. Poverty itself breeds indifference. Religion only sanctions that indifference by giving it a philosophical justification. India is not alone in her attitude. Most lands have, at one time or another, been faced with wretchedness and have accepted it philosophically for want of any other obvious way of acting. Upper-class Americans, during the Great Depression, were hardly more aggrieved over the Hooverville dwellers than Indians are over their slum folk. Volumes are written about Appalachia and black slums, yet it is not very hard to find well-off Americans who do not shed tears over them. In India it is a way of life to blink at the inhumanness of so many human lives. The pilgrims of Rishikesh feel no pity; the beggars want none. A coin is all they want, all they get.

However dehumanizing these attitudes may be, the beggars are nonetheless human. Gopal, the foot-clutching child beggar of Calcutta, laughs like any other boy. He weeps, eats and plays like any other boy. Gopal's life has the quality of a nightmare about it, but it has a carnival air, too. With his seven brothers and sisters and his four cousins, he roams the neighborhood like a mischievous puppy. Everything is fair game, from a grocery basket left untended for a moment to a garbage dump outside the bazaar, where crows and cows are fellow scavengers.

Begging is not a serious occupation for these children. If they want something and have no more-adventuresome means of getting it, they will hound some strollers or people waiting at a tram stop for the required coins. Only occasionally, if the men of the family are out of work for long and the need of the family is desperate, will they be sent out to beg seriously.

The barracks where Gopal's family lives stand by the side of a series of lakes and a park, reliable sources of fun and profit. Evening strollers, mellowed by the waters and the beauty of the surrounding park, are easy marks for begging. The lakes themselves provide food. Tiny fish are caught in old rags dipped into the water. The little minnows are dumped on the ground, where half-a-dozen children eagerly chase the jumping-creatures, snap off their heads and wrap up great heaps of them in other rags to take home and fry. At certain times of the year little shrimplike crawdads are dug out of the mud on the edges of the lakes. With potatoes and spices they make a curry fit for a beggar's feast.

The lakes are bathtub and washtub, kitchen basin and fishery, to the poor whose slums crowd nearby. From inside the wall of a fashionable boating club can be heard the slap slap slap of the washermen beating their laundry against flat stones. The splash of bathers clad in expensive swimming costumes is echoed by that of Gopal's mother washing herself and her only sari simultaneously.

Gopal is a regular swimmer. Once near the lake, he can never resist squirming out of his pants or shirt and leaping into the brown waters. His example always starts an avalanche of naked boys cascading into the water behind him. Gopal turns, ducks the nearest boy for a long few moments, laughingly splashes the others and a well-dressed stroller on shore as well, and bullfrogs out into deeper water. The boys seem unable to swim without ducking and splashing one another. More gentle forms of play rarely interest them.

Rough-and-tumble play is a way of life for them. After a wedding feast the parents of the bride court divine favor by tossing out bits and bones to the beggars who cluster near the scene. The children claw and fight one another for the scraps. Now and then they tear the coveted morsel into so many pieces that it can feed no one. These scrambles are ruthless and brutal. Yet a blindfolded passerby would guess from the sounds that nothing more terrible than gay play was afoot. Laughter and cheers ring out from the melee, which instantly dissolves, once all the food is gone, into comradely singing and a group departure for the next wedding in the neighborhood.

A measure of the gentle friendliness that is the opposite side of the coin to their roughhousing is the care Gopal and his brothers take of the younger children in the family. The little ones are always taken along on forays at the lake or to weddings. They are carefully provided with their quota of fish to mutilate, and the older children watch delightedly as the young ones scramble after their prey and gleefully snap off the heads.

Gopal is, of course, one of the lucky ones. His family has the barracks room. They and all their neighbors are squatters. Had they not claimed the building, it would have been demolished when the lake park was developed. But they had moved in uninvited, and no amount of urging would convince them to leave again.

Yet the shelter they gained is minimal. A tiny room about eight feet square is all they have, all eighteen of them. If they were really to live in their home, as Seema or Tinku do in theirs, they would crawl over it like lice on a monkey. The result could only be mutual suffocation. Instead, they use the room as a storage place for the cooking pots, for a couple of tin suitcases holding a change or two of clothes, for a few tiny clay idols and for dozens of vivid picture of divinities pinned to the walls.

The actual living of the family takes place outside. They bathe and wash dishes in the lakes. They cook in the park or on the pavements. They sleep on the ground or in the door-

ways of the bazaar several blocks away. The children especially, having been born on the streets, find it impossible to
sleep indoors. Only the most inclement weather will force
them to do so.

Yet inclement weather is the rule rather than the exception
in Calcutta. The monsoon is a long, wet one. Many inches
of water fall every day, day after day, night after night, for
four months. Intervals between storms are cloudy and humid.
Even those with luxurious homes feel thoroughly dampened
by the time dry weather reappears. Gopal and his family are
constantly drenched; they live like water creatures. Their
clothes grow moldy and rot on their bodies. Their scalps develop wet fungus. Their food is filled with insects.

Indeed, the six-footed life that thrives on the rain is more
of a burden than the water itself. Lice spring to life in the
slum people's hair, and constant scratching leads soon to
head sores. These wounds drain into the glands, and people
walk about stiff-necked, afraid to suffer the pain caused by
a glimpse to either side. Insects lay eggs under fingernails
and in ears. Frequent bathing is useless against these intruders: they glory in water. Other insects inhabit the air. Not
a meal passes without flying bugs landing in the food, which
was already maggoty anyway.

To sleep during these hot, rainy nights is a problem. Gopal
and most of his family prefer a doorway to the foulness of
the stuffy room. In drier times, the spirit of the pavements
is usually generous; there is always room for one more. But
the horrors of the monsoon shorten tempers. Fingers are
easily tramped on by newcomers to crowded corners, and
quarrels that come close to bloodshed are frequent.

In Delhi, pavement dwellers have less rain to worry them,
but more cold. Water never turns to ice on the plains during
a north Indian winter, yet the temperature in Delhi does

drop into the forties at night. That may not seem terribly cold to people who live with central heating, but even the well-to-do in Delhi do not have heat. They depend on quilts and woolens to keep them alive.

A score or so of the pavement dwellers do die of the cold each year. If wood can be found, huge fires are lighted on the streets, and people huddle close to warm themselves. But few can sleep close enough to the flames to benefit. The children of Delhi's streets scamper about, winter and summer, clad in thin cotton shirts. Not even on the coldest nights can many muster pants or shoes. A very lucky boy may pick up a moth-eaten scarf from a garbage heap. Whole families share the warmth of a single cotton shawl, and they huddle at night between the same thin covers that sheltered them from the sun during the summer.

Nevertheless, cold and rain are thought of as merely passing afflictions. It is really heat that is the poor man's burden. No one who has not sweated through an Indian summer without benefit of air-conditioning or electric fans or refrigerated water can begin to imagine the power of the tropical sun. Even warm water is often hard to come by for slum dwellers or the homeless who depend on a single slow-dripping, often dry water-tap in a neighborhood inhabited by thousands. These people do not sweat through the summers. They roast.

The adults of Gopal's family sleep away the long hot afternoons, with the infants snuggled close to them. It is the sleep of torpor. But Gopal and the other children fight the heat. All day they bathe in the lakes or gamble with stones beneath a shady tree. Only rarely do they crawl into a huge pipe or a cool ditch for an irresistible catnap. If once they sleep, they fear, they will lose the energy to play again.

Play and food are what seem important to Gopal. School

hardly figures in his life at all, although he is a student. His father enrolled his sons in a free government-school, and sometimes the children set out, slates under arms, in the general direction of the place. More often than not, though, they end up playing at the lake or begging by the tram stop or foraging in the garbage outside the market. At the age of eight, Gopal tucks his tongue thoughtfully into his cheek, bends his head to an inch above the slate, clenches his chalk in a tight fist and writes his name. He is proud of that accomplishment. He has no desire to learn more, not even to read his name written by someone else.

Gopal never thinks of his future, of how he'll live when he grows up, of what he would like to be. With a certainty born of his absolute inability to imagine anything else, he knows that he'll be a sometime-laborer like his father.

When a building goes up in the neighborhood, his father works. He sits in the hot sun, a pile of bricks at his side, a hammer in his hand. Slowly, as if time and his task had no end, he breaks the bricks into tiny pieces that will be mixed with concrete later. Sometimes he helps to lift pipes or he carries piles of bricks on his head up steep bamboo scaffolds. For a few weeks he was allowed to steady the ladder of a painter. With great pride he described himself as a *mistri*, a skilled worker. But then the painter's younger brother recovered from his fever, and Gopal's father went back to being a laborer. The easiest time of his adult life, a time he looks back on with head-shaking nostalgia, was a day or two when he was a strikebreaker. The pay, he remembers, was excellent, the work easy. All he had to do was walk into a factory with a large group of other men. But then the union picket-line formed and crossing it involved a fight. Gopal's father hastily resigned.

Gopal was once asked by a grim lady from whom he begged

ten *paise* what he planned to do when he grew up. He grinned unbelievingly, scratched his head and stretched his power of fantasy. All he could come up with was: "Maybe I'll get a license to pull a rickshaw. Or maybe I'll be a railway porter. I don't know. There'll be something."

6

Jewels for a Maharaja

WHEN YOGENDRA CHANDRA was eight years old, someone asked him, too, what he wanted to be when he grew up. Without hesitation he replied, "I'll be a pilot, or I'll design airplanes."

Aside from being eight and a child of India, Yogendra Chandra had nothing in common with the beggar Gopal—or for that matter with Tinku. But then, Yogendra Chandra is a prince. Rich and poor are extremes as old as history. Nowhere, though, are they quite so extreme as in India.

Mark Twain wrote a book called *The Prince and the Pauper*. Two boys, runs the tale, happened to meet. One was a young prince, the other a young pauper. Yet the two were as identical as twins. On a whim they determined to change places so that each might experience the life of the other. Mark Twain's story tells of their adventures.

In India the very supposition of such an exchange is unthinkable. No pauper could resemble a prince. Children of the poor are too uniformly thin and short, stunted by the lack of nutrients in their meager rice and *dal* diet. Princes feed on the best fruits and vegetables, on meat and fish and eggs if they are not vegetarians, on milk and butter and *ghee*. A prince meeting a pauper of his own age would probably look down on a boy several inches shorter and many pounds lighter than he.

Even if the two, having switched clothes, were miraculously to resemble each other, the signs of their stations would be too numerous to be hidden. Speech, expression, manner before adults, all would leap forth to reveal the deception.

Yogendra Chandra is today a man the age of Gopal's father. The latter is stooped and ladder-ribbed. Yogendra Chandra stands straight and broad in the chest. Both men wear moustaches, but the one Gopal's father wears tops cracked lips through which issue frequent dry coughs. Before any moderately well-dressed person Gopal's father bends his neck, drops his chin and speaks as little as possible. Yogendra Chandra is mild-mannered and polite to everyone, yet toward no one does he show anything less than a quiet sense of dignity, a dignity to be expected of the Raja of Jubbal.

When the British viceroy passed the symbols of power into the hands of Indian leaders in 1947, he gave over to them only three-quarters of the total area of the country. The rest had never legally been governed by England. It was held, instead, by princes, or rajas, 554 of them, ruling 554 separate kingdoms.

Actually, those kingdoms had not been truly independent during the days of the British Empire. The lands that the conquering Englishmen left unsubdued were those controlled by rulers who signed pacts giving power to the foreigners. At the right elbow of each raja sat an agent of the British government of India.

When independence came to India and Pakistan, the

princes had the choice of joining one of the two new nations or of declaring independence. Actually, no tiny state surrounded by a larger nation could truly remain free. So each raja merged his state, occasionally not without conflict, into India or Pakistan.

Those who joined India were deprived of the right to administer their states. But they were allowed to retain the titles of their rank, and they were awarded huge pensions, called privy purses, to make up for the loss of the tremendous fortunes they had derived from their kingdoms. Gradually the people of "democratic" India became more and more indignant over the special treatment accorded the princes, and the purses became the subject of furious debate. Today no realistic raja counts on receiving money from the government very much longer.

Are the rajas who are no longer rajas still regal? Do the men stripped of the means of power but endowed with its empty forms still have any authority?

In the persons of the young rajas who have never ruled are mixed many of the confusing, conflicting, chaotic elements of old-modern India. These men are advertising executives who return to their capitals of yore to don golden robes and lead stately processions at festival times. They are manufacturers of modern electronic equipment who hurry to the halls of Parliament to beg a bridge or a new irrigation pump for their subjects of yesterday. They are back-room party bosses who derive power from the authority of their former sizable states and who make the political princes of today.

Jubbal, which Yogendra Chandra's family once ruled, is a fairyland kingdom high in the Himalayas. Its rulers long lived in three palaces perched on hilltops and seemingly spun from the airy timber of fantasy. Towers and gables sit lightly on boxy wings that rise from the roofs of rooms farther down the hillside. Stairways wind crazily from sitting rooms to bed-rooms. Kitchens and servants' quarters lie at the base. One of these three wooden palaces was lost in a recent fire. The other two stand and are lived in still.

"As children, we used to ride three days on horseback to get from the town of Simla to Jubbal, sixty miles to the northeast," says Yogendra Chandra. "Now we drive it in three hours."

Improved transport has boosted the economy of Jubbal, although the raja claims that it was always one of the wealth-iest spots in Asia. Timber, apples and seed potatoes are its crops. Its people live in scattered villages lost in the forests and orchards. The town of Jubbal itself houses less than a thousand souls. It is a mere center of administration and marketing.

Until 1947 Jubbal was a kingdom. Now it is one of twenty-two former kingdoms that make up a single district of the state of Himachal Pradesh. Yogendra Chandra has never ruled. His father supervised the transfer of power to New Delhi and then concentrated upon directing family farms and investments. His only son, Yogendra Chandra, was ten years old at the time New Delhi took over. For five years already he had lived in boarding schools far away from his family. He barely knew Jubbal in the days of its independence, and he never had any thought of ruling it.

Through his years at school he did not mention his princely heritage. "Most of my classmates never knew I was from a ruling family. I wasn't at all embarrassed about it, but neither did I want it to be widely known."

Like most other boys, Yogendra Chandra had his ambitious dream. The world of flying enchanted him, and he wanted above all else to become a pilot, to join the Indian Air Force and perhaps to learn the basics of aeronautical design. But like all other boys, Yogendra Chandra had a mother. Being a rani, a queen, as well, did nothing to lessen her anxiety for her son. No, said she firmly. You shall not fly. You shall not join the Air Force. You shall not have anything to do with those dangerous devils called airplanes. Probably, thoughts of the unsuitability of a prince's concerning himself with technical matters also influenced her opposition.

The young heir to the kingdom of Jubbal, which was no more a kingdom, mourned in private. But he was an Indian son of an Indian family, and he accepted the decision of his elders. He enrolled in a liberal arts course, passed his college years without enthusiasm and prepared himself to inherit not a kingdom, not a future, but a business.

Three farms in different parts of the mountains and foothills are the heart of his inheritance. The Raja of Jubbal grows paddy, wheat, sugarcane and fruit. In addition he owns shares in movie houses and hotels.

"But I don't like business, and I don't like agriculture," sighs Yogendra Chandra. "I might be more interested in farming if I had been allowed to take a course in agricultural sciences. But my parents wouldn't agree to my taking up any technical line."

Gopal the beggar boy feels no dissatisfaction with his place in the world. But the Raja of Jubbal breathes dissatisfaction about his. He feels he has accomplished little. "All these businesses were my father's before they were mine. I've started nothing."

But if Gopal is free from disappointment, he is equally free from hope. The Raja of Jubbal, on the other hand, has plenty of that. "Now I'm working on a project which is another tale entirely," he says with quiet pride. "We are about to start building a factory to produce polyethylene bags." With a smile he adds, "There's some fascinating engineering involved.

It will only be a small factory at first, but modern, up-to-date, and mine."

Yogendra Chandra would seem to be a young man wholly engaged by the world of today. But he is also the Raja of Jubbal.

In 1970 the New Delhi government tried to cancel the princely allowances. Shortly afterward Yogendra Chandra returned to Jubbal for the important holiday Dussehra. Hitherto, he had always led the procession and lighted the firecracker-filled effigies of the demons, just as his ancestors had done before him. That year, he thought the custom might have finally come to an end.

"My people came to me," he remembers, "and said, 'Those people in Delhi may have taken away your purse and your titles, but they haven't taken you from our hearts.' I led the procession just as I had always done."

The feudal flavor of princely concern for one's subjects hangs heavily about the Raja of Jubbal. "I feel responsible for my people. I take up their needs with government and speak for them whenever I can.

"I haven't the time to be truly involved in politics, to stand for Parliament or the state legislature. But I wish I could. I wish I could really represent my people."

Businessman, agriculturist, engineer, entrepreneur, prince-without-sanction, Yogendra Chandra is also a family man. When he was twenty-three, his parents arranged his marriage to the Princess of Keonthal, another pocket kingdom in the mountains. He had known his elegant bride since childhood. The princely families that abounded in the area formed a social coterie of their own. Frequent intermarriage had united the ruling families even more closely; the Raja and Rani of Jubbal, for instance, are distantly related cousins.

Three girls were born to the royal couple. They live most

of the year in a large house in Simla, a mountain resort town not far from Delhi. *Ayahs* attend to the children; their mother leaves the details of their upbringing in the hands of servants, while she herself stays close by and supervises.

Says the Raja of Jubbal, "I think all children should be free to make their own decisions about their own lives. Parents should never force their youngsters to do what they would otherwise not choose to do.

"But," he quickly adds, "*if* I have any opportunity to advise my daughters, I hope that one will become a lawyer, another a nuclear physicist, and the third an aeronautical designer.

"Of course, this is still India," he concludes with a shy grin. "They'll probably all be married and become nothing more than mothers."

Here the attractive Rani of Jabbal nods sharply. She is not a partisan of modern theories about bringing up daughters. "Naturally, parents should arrange marriages for their girls! Who else will see to it that they are properly married?" Yogendra Chandra's wife has lined the walls of their Simla home with portraits of royal ancestors. She makes certain that her girls know who the people in those pictures are, how they are related, what their titles are.

Although the Rani of Jubbal leans more sharply toward princely tradition than does her husband, she does not bypass the twentieth century altogether. An acquaintance, an official of Simla, urged her to begin cultivating mushrooms two years ago. Mushrooms are not a traditional food in India, and they have been introduced only recently in small, highly priced tins. The Rani pondered, decided she would like to have a new interest of her own and took up the challenge. Today she grows an impressive crop of mushrooms, which she sells to the government to be canned. She is planning with her husband to begin canning her own crop soon. They are making plans for a modern plant.

Both Yogendra Chandra and his wife span two eras. They make no apologies for the foot on the side of the past. Yet the Raja of Jubbal is also a realistic man. He looks ahead and wonders what the adult lives of his daughters will be. Will they still be princesses? Or will they be ordinary individuals with nothing more distinctive about them than colorful childhood memories of faces in portraits lining the walls of their parents' home? The Raja of Jubbal deeply hopes that his girls will be immersed in the present century. Yet just as deeply does he mourn the probable passing of the princely heritage.

Today there are no more jewels for the Raja of Jubbal. The fabled riches of princes have not, however, passed into the hands of the beggars. A not-so-magic wand has changed them instead into the luxury cars and glass mansions of the new princes: the upper-crust politicians, the new-generation industrialists and the black-market traders. Unless a mighty revolution overtakes the current drift of events, rich and poor seem destined to mark the social seas of India for a long time to come. That division might not be so troubling if the rich were not quite so rich, if the poor were not so very dreadfully poor. But the deep gap separating the two has grown over the long centuries of India's history, and is not today to be easily wished away.

7

Caste

LAKSHMI is a maidservant for the Krishnamurtis, who occupy a tiny flat in Madras. Mr. Krishnamurti works as an accounting clerk in the office of the Controller of Imports and Exports. There are five Krishnamurti children, the eldest a girl of nine, the youngest a girl of three months.

As Mrs. Krishnamurti grinds spices for the afternoon curry, Lakshmi scrubs the pots on the kitchen floor. "Has your baby gotten over his cough?" asks Mrs. K.

"He has," replies Lakshmi, vigorously applying ashes from the stove to shine the surface of a brass frying-pan. "I gave him some ground ginger mixed with warm water, and he was over it in no time. Why don't you try it for Arupa?"

The chatter proceeds as between equals while the work goes on. After a while Lakshmi rinses her pan from a bucket of water, straightens up and groans. "I'm ready for tea now," she announces. As Mrs. Krishnamurti pours out two cups, Lakshmi retires to the landing outside the door. Mrs. K. takes the servant's cup out to her; it is a cracked cup used only by

Lakshmi. Mrs. K. returns to the kitchen to sip her own tea.

"Sonia was telling me she cooks a curry of cauliflower and carrots," calls out Lakshmi. "Have you ever made it that way?" The conversation continues through the doorway.

However much the two women may share each other's lives and problems, they would never consider drinking tea in the same room. For Lakshmi's caste is lower than the Krishnamurtis'.

Long, long ago—nobody knows just when or how—Hindu society was marked off into divisions called castes. These divisions overlap and honeycomb the one between the rich and the poor, and they are at least as durable. Originally, each caste was defined by the occupation of its male members. *Brahmins* were priests, *Kshatriyas* rulers and warriors, *Vaisyas* traders and bankers, *Sudras* farmers. Those were, and still are, the four main castes. Outside them stood the *pariahs*, the people who cleaned the drains and ditches of their neighbors, who handled dead animals and did whatever other tasks were thought to be unclean. Because their work was considered by Hindus to be defiling, the outcastes who did it were considered to be defiled. Offal could not be touched by a pious Hindu; neither could the men and women who touched it. Thus, the members of this lowest segment of society were *ausprishaw* ("untouchable").

Nobody really knows the history of caste or how it changed from a naming of jobs to a ranking of social positions. All that is certain is that the change happened. The *Brahmin*, who never used physical strength, who occupied himself with spiritual matters and kept happy the all-powerful gods and goddesses, stood highest in the social order. *Sudras*, on the other hand, were concerned with the sweaty task of filling men's bellies and so stood at the bottom of the caste hierarchy.

In time each caste became entwined in a plethora of rules and rituals: *Brahmins* may not eat food prepared by lower-caste people. *Brahmin* boys must pass through an initiation ceremony at puberty and thereafter wear a thread across their chest. Castes may not intermarry. The child of one caste belongs to that caste and no other. The rules were infinitely multiplied.

As the strange plant of caste put out longer and stronger roots, the four stems divided and subdivided. Buds appeared on the new branches, and more twigs grew from the buds. The result today is a system of subcastes so numerous that serious scholars devote their lives to untangling the confusion of castes in small areas of the country.

The growth of divisions must have occurred along with another change. Somewhere along the line, probably so slowly that people did not notice, caste became divorced from the classification of jobs that had spawned it. Today *Brahmins* still tend to be found more among the higher levels of society than the lower. But a modern *Brahmin* may be a landlord, a farmer, a maidservant, a banker, a writer, a vendor of vegetables, or almost anything else. A twentieth-century *Sudra* may collect rent from a *Kshatriya* tenant. A *Vaisya* shop assistant may toss bolts of cloth to his *Kshatriya* employer.

What, then, is caste today? That is a tricky question. It is easier by far to list the things caste is not. Caste is not a system of occupations, although people from the same caste tend to bunch around the same jobs. It is not a network of political forces, although politicians, particularly in south India, often take alert notice of caste sentiments and loyalties. It is not solely a religious ritual, for it dictates and permeates the whole social structure of India. Nor is it simply a sociological phenomenon, for it is intimately bound up with the religious and philosophical existence of Hindus.

For western students, the psychological nature of caste is probably its most baffling aspect. Every land has some ranking of social position. In the United States, for instance, two major rankings cut across all others: the economic and the racial. A poor man stands below a rich man, a black man (at least until this generation) below a white man. Every American assumes that those valuations are loaded with emotion. The poor man feels ashamed, guilty, worthless, inferior, because he is poor. In the past the black man often accepted the disdain of the white man and turned it against himself. He tried to erase the signs of his blackness, to straighten his hair and to lighten his color. He considered himself to be shiftless and unimportant because the bigoted white man thought him so.

It is difficult, then, for an American to understand that the Indian system of rank, complex and permeating as it is, is very largely free from self-doubt. A lower-caste man accepts all the signs and rituals of his social inferiority to a *Brahmin*. Yet not for a moment does he *feel* that he is a less worthy human being. He is lower on the social ladder; he therefore owes to the *Brahmin* certain unquestioned dignities and privileges. But those rituals in no way reflect on his own dignity or sense of happiness with himself. He feels no anger, no guilt, no resentment, no self-hatred, because he was born into a lower caste, although he may take pains to try to raise the position of that caste a notch or two. His religion tells him that he was born where he was because of the deeds and misdeeds of his previous life. For the deeds of the person he was before he existed in his present form, he cannot feel any responsibility.

The one exception—and it is a profound one—is in the case of the *pariahs*, those who are *ausprishaw* or untouchable. Toward them the caste Hindus project all their own aversion toward what is unclean. The caste Hindu shrinks from a *pariah* he meets on the road; the touch of his very shadow is defiling to a south Indian *Brahmin*. *Pariahs* are denied the dignity of being accepted as fully human, a dignity accorded members of even the lowest caste, and the *pariahs* cannot escape incorporating a certain measure of that attitude into their sense of self.

Caste is like a magic stone: it is a hard fact of Indian life, yet it turns to water when one tries to grasp it. Caste is different in every village. And India has more than half a million villages. Rules vary. Some subcastes are found in one village only; others are spread over thousands of places. Family and clan identities overlap and confuse the picture. Rituals are not only different in different villages; sometimes they are directly opposite.

In the little village of Bajitpur, in the little corner of that long house where Tinku's family lives, caste is as important as it is anywhere, and as unique.

Tinku's family are *Brahmins*. Only one visible sign advertises this fact. The men and the boys over twelve wear over one shoulder and under the other arm a thin thread, the symbol of their having undergone a coming-of-age ceremony. In south India caste may often be read from the finger-painted marks on a person's head. Some central Indian castes tattoo marks on their forearms. The men of others allow a single lock of hair at the crown of the head to grow very long as a caste sign. But such symbols are not customary among Bengalis, and they are absent from the house in Bajitpur.

Obedience to the rules of caste, however, is nonetheless rigid. The *Sudra* peasant maidservant has her own chipped cup from which to drink tea. When the tenants are served a meal to celebrate the harvest festival each year, they are seated in the courtyard rather than on the kitchen veranda, and they eat not from the family's brass platters but from banana leaves cut into large squares. Tinku's grandmother performs her *Brahmin puja,* or devotions, twice a day as well as observing special fasts and *puja* once a week.

Tinku's uncle wished to marry a girl who lived nearby. It seemed an entirely suitable match. The girl was cheerful and intelligent. She shared with Tinku's uncle, whom she'd known all her life, most of his likes and dislikes. She was skilled in the arts of housekeeping. She was loved by the bridegroom's mother as well as by the bridegroom. And she was also a *Brahmin.* The marriage did not take place. The girl's subcaste, said the priest, was not only different from that of Tinku's family; it was one with which they were specifically forbidden to intermarry.

Tinku's family may eat duck eggs, but not chicken eggs; goat meat, but not lamb; fish, but not poultry. Other subcastes permit their members to eat chicken eggs, but not duck eggs; vegetables that grow inside the ground, but not those, like cauliflower or eggplant, that grow above it; meat, but not fish. The only universal Hindu law is that beef is forbidden to all.

Tinku's family are kindly people. They would not willingly hurt another fellow-being. Yet their caste laws demand of them specific cruelties toward those who are *ausprishaw.* They will not allow anyone *ausprishaw* to draw water from their well or to enter the village temple. They will not enter an *ausprishaw*'s house or treat an *ausprishaw* with any of the customary hospitality in their own home.

Modern people in New Delhi claim that caste is dying. They cite the fact that their household servant, who fifteen years ago would never clean the bathroom, now does so. Tremendous influxes of migrants to the city have in fact squeezed some of the juice out of caste prejudices. If a green peasant is so hungry that he will agree to do all the work in a house, cleaning bathrooms included, so that his master needn't hire a special outcaste for the purpose, then that peasant will obviously be preferred for the job. The more traditional servant can only compete by relenting and doing likewise. Often, though, the bias is too ingrained, and the person would rather not work than give in.

Political movements have also greatly improved the legal situation of the *Harijans,* the "people of God," as Gandhi dubbed them. It is now against the law to deny entrance to a temple to anyone. *Harijans* are supposed to be free to enter any public eating-place or hotel. They may not legally be handicapped in applying for any job.

In fact, though, the law is largely ignored. Outcastes may now be *Harijans,* but they still more often than not do *ausprishaw* work. In Bajitpur they skin the dead cattle, clean drains, sweep the roads. Untouchability, however firmly outlawed it might be in the archives of Parliament, is very much alive in the Bajitpurs of India.

8

Religion

IN INDIA, as everywhere, routine is both the balm and the bogeyman of the ordinary person's life. Day after day children attend the same schools or drive the same cattle to graze. Women cook the same sorts of foods at the same times. Men till the same fields or race their motorbikes along the same streets on the way to the same offices.

Without an occasional break in the routine, monotony might lead to madness. How welcome is that rare trip to the cinema! How exciting is the coming of sound trucks and banners at electiontime!

But movies and horn-blowing elections are offshoots of the twentieth century. The ancient people of India depended on something else to spice their lives with variety: religion and its festivals. Today more modern forms of entertainment may compete with the pull of the traditional holidays, but nothing has displaced it. Indians sometimes imagine that their forefathers celebrated the festivals with more color, more verve, more *élan,* than is ever seen today. Yet plenty of all three still remain in the festivals of the land.

India is like an immense attic crammed with the accumulated religious lore of many centuries and many places. The variety is overwhelming. Each region and religion has its own calendar of holidays. There are so many that it is difficult to decide where to begin describing them.

Let us look first at one of those best loved by the people of Kerala, at the southernmost tip of India. Kerala is a long, thin coastal state. Endless groves of coconut trees wave their fronds over placid lagoons from which reflect dancing sparks of sunshine. Long beaches fanned by tropical palms peacefully frame an interior rich in rubber and tea. The people of Kerala are the most literate in India, and also among the poorest.

In this lush land there is a religious festival celebrated yearly with great pride and warmth. It is . . . Christmas! Every fifth person in Kerala is Christian. While the greatest concentration of them is in Kerala, Christians are scattered throughout India. But those elsewhere are Roman Catholics or Protestants, converts within the last two hundred years of Europeans and Americans who came as missionaries. The Kerala Christians, on the other hand, are an ancient community. Tradition has it that Thomas Didymus, one of the twelve apostles of Jesus, came to Kerala in A.D. 52 and began the original seven churches. The Christians of the region are today members of the Syrian church, with rituals and masses that combine some orthodox elements with others that have evolved on the spot over the centuries.

The Christians of Kerala sense no conflict between their religion and their nationality. The women wear saris and bangles. When speaking to other Indians, they refer to their religious practices as *puja*. A Christian woman praising a Hindu child to his mother is apt to remark, "Of course he's bright; he's a *Brahmin*, after all."

Local conditions have likewise caused many differences in the forms with which holidays are celebrated in Kerala. There are no evergreens for Christmas trees. Poverty makes the exchange of gifts on Christmas Day impractical. Instead, Kerala Christians celebrate mass, then go to visit friends and relatives, who feed them traditional cakes and sweets. People sit beneath the palms on balmy Christmas nights singing carols in their mother tongue, Malayalam.

Far more numerous than Christians in India today are the Muslims. The ancestors of most Muslims were Hindus, often outcastes or residents of the poorest villages. In the eighth century Muslim armies came from the West and gradually conquered most of India. The religion of the new rulers promised to the most hopeless people of the land a life in which caste inequalities had no place and in which the Hindus, even the mightiest *Brahmins*, could be considered inferiors floundering outside the one true religion.

For centuries Hindus and Muslims in India lived peacefully side by side. Often they inhabited the same villages and neighborhoods. Hinduism traditionally accepts all other religions as valid, and the Indian Muslims, with the blood of their tolerant Hindu ancestors in their veins, were more interested in living with peace and dignity than in converting nonbelievers. Then suddenly in the twentieth century the mood changed. Hindus became outraged that Muslim beef-eaters slaughtered holy cows. Muslims became irritated at noisy Hindu processions outside their mosques when the devout were praying. Such petty excuses were enough to set Muslims and Hindus to massacring one another. Whole communities were sometimes wiped out in these communal holocausts.

Obviously, a bit of noise or a slaughtered cow is not really sufficient cause for such slaughter. Some Indians blame the British for whipping up trouble. An axiom of imperial rule was to "divide and rule," and the nationalists claim that the British applied it by goading Muslims and Hindus to despise one another. Others reason that however much the British may have encouraged divisions, they could never have created any as passionate as these unless some other, far deeper, causes were also at work.

People in India, so dormant and unstirred for centuries, are today being pulled and prodded by the modern industrial age. Factories and their benefits may not be visible; they may exist only thousands of miles away. Yet their social tentacles produce in the backward slums and villages of India a deeply disturbing bewilderment. Age-old ways are threatened. The thick psychic armor behind which people protect their raw selves from the wretchedness of poverty and hopelessness grows thin and brittle. People react with blind terror; undirected, that fear turns to hate, and the hate is spilled out in burning torrents against the neighbors who are "different," yet not so different that they can resist attack. Thus are born the brutal melees in which so many Hindus and Muslims have died.

These communal outbursts, however, are sporadic. In between, people exercise their Indian capacity for forgetting and forgiving, and join together to share the joys of one another's festivals.

Id-ul-Fitr is one of the major Muslim ones. Id celebrates the end of the Muslim month of Ramzan. Many regional and religious communities in India follow their own calendars, each one different from all the others. The Muslim calendar follows the moon. A month ends every time the moon is full. Muslim holidays thus fall every year on a different day of the national solar calendar.

Whenever it comes, Id-ul-Fitr is celebrated joyfully. During the month of Ramzan, says Muslim lore, the holy book of the religion, called the Koran, was revealed to the prophet Muhammad. The faithful fast every day of Ramzan, forgoing certain foods altogether and refusing any nourishment during the daylight hours. When the month ends and Id-ul-Fitr is observed, Muslims assemble in huge numbers at their mosques and holy places for prayer. Like the Kerala Christians on Christmas Day, they cap their prayers with visits. People troop cheerfully to the homes of their friends, Hindu as well as Muslim, carrying gifts of food and sharing the embrace that typifies the occasion.

Christianity and Islam are two religions that came to India from other lands. Many other creeds have similarly taken root in the land. In Cochin, a southern coastal town of Kerala, a community of Jews resides. One of their number, a young woman, visited the United States and there met an American lady whose grandparents had fled anti-Semitic persecution in Europe sixty years before.

"How long have your people lived in India?" asked the American, with the event of her own ancestors' migration fresh in her memory.

Replied the Indian girl coolly, "Three thousand years."

The estimate may have been exaggerated, but not by much. The first group of Jewish settlers is said to have arrived in Kerala during the sixth century B.C. More came in the first century A.D., when Roman persecution drove them from Jerusalem. Others arrived at various other times over the centuries. But today the community has almost vanished. Many migrated to Holland and England during colonial days. More recently, a few have gone to Israel.

Another, more recent, group of religious refugees, though, is flourishing in its adopted land. These people are the Parsis, who live mainly in Bombay. The Tatas, India's greatest industrialists, are among the best-known members of this community. The success and wealth of the Tatas are extreme, but the family itself is representative of the Parsi norm. They are known to be forward-looking, advanced, enlightened, cultured people. Almost alone among Indian businessmen they advocate practices revolutionary for India: fixed prices instead of haggling, straightforward contracts instead of shady deals.

The Parsis are Zoroastrians, a religion stigmatized by outsiders as the creed of fire worshipers. The most primitive religions known to anthropologists also taught men to worship fire, water and the other elements, and so Zoroastrians are generally believed to be primitive animists of that type. Actually, their philosophy is considerably more complex and sophisticated. Zoroastrians are monotheists, believing in a single god whose blinding glory and generous abundance are best symbolized by fire and water. Their divinity teaches them to follow a path of good thoughts and good deeds, especially of service to others. Concern for the community is thus a religious dictum.

Because the elements are sacred, Parsis do not bury or burn their dead. To do so would defile either fire or earth, they believe. Instead, they build high towers, called Towers of Silence, and leave the corpses on the top to be eaten by vultures. The Tower of Silence in Bombay is one of the sights always pointed out—from a distance!—to visitors. Another is the special well from which the Parsis draw all the water they drink. The water is carried on horse-drawn wooden carts and delivered daily to the city's Parsi households.

Unlike the Zoroastrians, Christians, Muslims and Jews, most of the remaining religious minorities in India are not imports but offshoots of Hinduism. The Sikhs, for instance, who live primarily in Punjab, belong to a sect that rebelled against caste four hundred years ago. Sikh men are the most easily recognizable group in India. They never shave or cut their hair. They pull their locks into topknots on the crown of the head, secure them with wooden combs and then cover them with elaborately wound turbans in vivid colors. On one wrist they wear an iron bangle. Long hair and bangles might suggest effeminacy. But the abundantly bearded Sikh men are usually tall and well-built, and they are supposed to be warlike and courageous. One of the original symbols of their sect was a long sword, which was always to be carried by the mature men. Today the sword has dwindled to a tiny concealed one, but the symbolism remains.

In the western states of India are concentrated members of another, much older, offshoot of Hinduism. These are the Jains, noted for their pacifism. To a Jain, all life is sacred, however tiny or insignificant its form. Strict vegetarians, devout Jains sweep the path on which they walk with a soft broom lest they inadvertently step on a creature too small to be seen.

The best known of the children of Hinduism is Buddhism. It is also the most widely exported, being the dominant religion today of many Asian lands: Burma, Ceylon, Japan, Vietnam and others. Buddha was a Hindu prince who, stunned by the suffering of people all around him, renounced his station in life. Sitting beneath a large banyan tree, he meditated on the ugliness that had so shaken him. From where does evil spring? he pondered. Why is man afflicted by illness, grief, poverty and loss? How can the generations be freed from their headlong rush into a world of misery?

He never doubted that each generation was doomed by the ones before to live in wretchedness. That is implicit in the Hindu doctrine of reincarnation, the rebirth of souls. People, according to this belief, die only to be born again in some other form or station. One may be reborn as a prince or as a frog. Which it is will be determined by how well one performed one's fate-appointed duty in the previous life.

Sitting under that banyan tree at Bodh-Gaya, Buddha believed that he had received enlightenment, that he had found a way out of the cycle of death and rebirth. All evil, all wrong-doing, he thought, sprang from desire. If a man desired nothing, he would do nothing but what his duty dictated. The religious task of man was, therefore, to free himself from desire, and Buddha believed he might do so through meditation. Once rid of all desire, all fear, all involvement, the soul of the meditator would then merge with the cosmic unity. In other words, his soul, or life-energy, or whatever one chooses to call the element that makes a person or a frog an entity separate from all others, would cease to be separate. Buddha saw the state of not-being, which he called *nirvana*, as the acme of blessedness, free from all passions, whether sorrowful or joyful.

To people who are more or less well-fed, who live far from the maddening realities of Indian-style wretchedness, the aloofness that is the Buddhist ideal is very foreign. Why should a living human being want to give up the joys of life in order to rid himself of the woes? Even brief tastes of love, of achievement or of creativity should be ample reward for the pains of living.

The difficulty is that poverty, illness and the absence of hope make even fleeting experiences of happiness rare in India. Life is so regulated by immovable custom, so lacking in the unexpected, so much richer in disaster than in success, that people find the promise of *nirvana* to be more real and satisfying than that of human joy. It is thus not strange that India produced Buddha. It is far more curious that so few Indians embrace Buddhism, that most of the followers of Buddha live in other lands.

If Buddhism took little hold on the minds of the masses of

Hindus, it was because the parent creed is as warm, as broad, as human and as full of promise as the mythological Mother herself. Whatever a person's station, whatever his intellect or his inclinations, he can embrace some aspect of Hinduism.

To a westerner, Hinduism suggests mysticism. Yogis practice ancient exercises in breathing and body control in order to attain rarified spiritual heights. *Sadhus,* the naked or saffron-clad monks who roam the countryside, are reputed to achieve strange mystical experiences. Mysticism is indeed an integral part of the religion. Yet it is one with which the ordinary man has little to do.

He is also little involved with the profound and complex philosophy of Hinduism. The unity of all things is the essence of that belief. Every creature, every plant, every vapor and wave of energy is unique. Yet all are related and bound together, for each is simply a different reflection of a supreme spirit. Like an omnipotent prism, the divine One sends off one ray of being that is Man, another that is Earth, another that is all other Life. The ordinary Hindu, however, rarely meditates on the oneness of all creation. He is far more involved in the religious axioms that derive from the basic precepts. Chief among these is the belief in rebirth. Each person has a *dharma,* a role in life, according to his birth. If he lives strictly within the bounds of that role, if he never rebels but performs all the duties and deeds of his position, then he will be reborn in a higher station. To obey one's *dharma* is the doctrine of *karma.* It offers the Hindu a simple hope, never testable in his lifetime. More, it offers him a cast-iron set of rules with which he may govern his life. Caste is, in a sense, a social solidification of *karma.*

For a man who has been born a warrior, a *Kshatriya,* it is right and good to fight in a war. For the *Sudra,* or farmer, who lives next door to that warrior, it is just as right and good to ignore the war and to reap his harvest. If a stray blow should fell the farmer, the warrior will not feel it necessary to reap the grain. If the enemy, on the other hand, should occupy the farmer's village, the *Sudra* will not consider the possibility of resisting him. Warrior and farmer, each has his ordained function, his fated role. The warrior expects to be reborn a prince if he bears arms. But the farmer who kills an enemy encamped in his village fears that he will emerge as a snake in the next existence.

Religious concepts such as *karma* shade off into a body of ritual and custom deeply embedded in the life style of the ordinary Hindu. When a woman must cook, when she must conceive a baby, how she should dress and eat once her husband has died; where a man should bathe and what occupation he must pursue; when a baby should first eat solid foods and when his hair should first be cut; all are decisions to be made not according to logic or personal inclination, but by religious rule.

Cleanliness, for instance, is one of the central tenets of Hinduism. But it is more a ritual cleanliness than a real one. The Hindu must bathe in a body of water in which he can immerse himself. The nearest such body may be a polluted pond or a muddy river. The devout Hindu will pass by buckets of clear well-water in his own home on his way to "clean" himself in one of these "holy" bodies of water.

Food that has come in contact with another human's mouth is contaminated. The Hindu cook never, never tests the saltiness of her curry by sipping from her ladle. If, however, a potato hops out of the pot and falls in the ashes, that same cook sees nothing wrong in picking it up, dusting it off and tossing it right back in again. A pious *Brahmin* may not eat food cooked by a woman who is menstruating. Nowhere does it say, though, that he should not drink the milk into which his tubercular wife has coughed.

Other Hindu attitudes are also more symbolic than actual. Cows are sacred, proclaims the potbellied vegetable vendor. That cow, he shrieks in the next breath, that cow is eating my carrots. And he lets go a barrage of stones and kicks.

We hold women to be divine, explains the serene Hindu husband, for all womanhood is the manifestation of the mother goddess. Wife! he yells. I'm thirsty from talking. Bring me a glass of water!

However unreal such tenets may be, there is at least one for virtually every occasion in everyday Hindu life. There are dozens relating to food. To offer the gods sweets and fruit as a sign of reverence for them is a firm religious rule. No less firm is the rule that food must be offered to a visitor. The gods are pleased with edible offerings. The gods are manifestations of a divine unity that includes all beings. The visitor is yet another reflection of that same One. The visitor, too, must be welcomed and propitiated by food. That dictum is happily reinforced by the warm interest most of the people of India feel toward a stranger.

The stuff of hospitality also relates back to another Hindu tenet. The cow is sacred largely because the abundance of her milk suggests that she is an incarnation of the mother spirit; the human mother is also a giver of nurturing milk, and the divine mother is the bestower of all that is humanly good. Logically, then, milk is the stuff of which the sweets traditionally offered both to goddesses and visitors are made. *Ghee*, clarified butter, is also an essential both in the temple and in the kitchen.

Yet here we can glimpse another aspect of Hinduism: its flexibility. Milk is the stuff of divine hospitality. But people may be too poor to feed their idols and guests rich sweets and *ghee*. For the poor, a banana and a glass of water are just as acceptable signs of hospitality and devotion as are more expensive foods for the wealthy.

Almost every "firm" rule of Hinduism is allowed some exceptions. Even the despised outcastes, barred from the premises of holy places all year long, are allowed to enter the caste temples on Kali Puja day. Yet nowhere is the quality of Hinduism more startling than in the release it offers the ordinary worshiper from the rigorous Oneness of its philosophy. The divine spirit may be one, but its manifestations are many: as many as the waves, as many as the stars, as many as the individuals who together comprise mankind, as many, in fact, as the gods and goddesses whose images people the altars of Hinduism.

Brahma the Creator, Shiva the Destroyer and Vishnu the Preserver are the three major gods. Hindu mythology has created for each a battery of wives, sons and daughters. Each, moreover, may take many guises. Vishnu, for instance, appears on earth in a different incarnation whenever the world is threatened by evil.

It was one of those incarnations, Rama, that gave to India the epic *Ramayana*. It is Rama also who provides for the Hindus of north India one of the major festivals of the year: Dussehra.

Rama, one of four princes, was born to destroy Ravana, the demon king of a distant island. Through the wiles of a jealous queen, Rama was exiled to the forest with his wife, Sita, and his brother Laksman. There Sita was captured by Ravana and carried away to his island fortress. After a series of adventures and with the help of an army of monkeys commanded by the manlike monkey-god Hanuman, Rama eventually won back his wife. Dussehra celebrates this story. Each night for ten nights masked and colorfully costumed dancers re-create the Rama legend in the parks and market squares of the towns and cities. Sita yearns for a golden deer, really wicked Ravana in disguise, and is led to her undoing. Hanuman, gone to Ravana's kingdom to reconnoiter and captured by demons who set his tail on fire, burns down the enemy's capital city, Lanka. Monkeys leap rapturously in battle with demons, who finally fall and die. At the end of the tenth day's dance, when Sita has been recaptured and Lanka destroyed, huge firecracker-filled effigies of Ravana are ignited, and the final gala is celebrated with bursting rockets and booming bombs.

Dessehra is celebrated differently in different places. In Bengal it is not Rama but the goddess Durga who is worshiped. Durga is the mother goddess, but she is also the goddess of war. It was through her grace that Rama won his battle with Ravana. Her image in Bengal is that of a sweet-faced, elegantly attired lady. She has ten arms. Some of her plump hands hold feminine objects, such as musical instruments. But others clutch fearful weapons. One is a long spear, its point embedded in the chest of a man who lies bleeding at the goddess's feet. From the wound pours blood and gore.

Hindus find no contradiction in the dual aspect of Durga: mother and warrior. Mother is the conqueror of evil. Evil is embodied in demons like the fearful Ravana. How can Durga combat evil if she is not armed? On another level, though, there is much to be read in the concept of Woman with Man bleeding at her feet. Durga Puja in Bengal is, in fact, the one occasion when women emerge from their kitchens to claim an event as their own. Clad in new saris, which every woman demands for the Puja, the ladies flock to neighborhood altars where community committees have set up images of the goddess. Priests chant to the beat of big drums. Incense is lighted and food-stuffs are laid before the image. After four days the goddess is carried in noisy procession to a river or pond and there immersed in water so that the clay of the particular image may rejoin the generality of clay from which it was originally taken.

Durga is one of the consorts of Shiva. Another is Parvati, the goddess of fertility. Parvati receives little attention in most of India, where fertility is generally not a problem. But her son, Ganesh, is one of the most widely admired, and one of the most engaging, of the Hindu pantheon. Ganesh is the pot-bellied impish creature—man from the neck down, elephant above—whose statue we met leaning against the cowshed in Bajitpur. Many legends are told to explain Ganesh's peculiarities. Each area, each community, has its own, and each is tailored to the characteristics and needs of the people who tell it.

One day, runs one myth, Parvati told Ganesh to sit by the door and keep everyone from entering while she had her bath. Shiva, who had been out, returned to find his entrance barred by his own young son; after all, Mother had said *everyone* should be kept out. Enraged, Shiva chopped off Ganesh's head. When Parvati emerged from her bath to find her mutilated son, she was heartbroken. Wailing, she begged her husband, by then thoroughly repentant, to remedy the damage. Shiva agreed to replace the severed head with that of the next creature to happen by. And along came an elephant.

Another myth has it that Parvati and Shiva were long child-less before Ganesh's arrival. No parents were every happier than they at the birth of a beautiful son. When the time came for the baby to eat his first rice, the usual ceremony was planned. One minor goddess, however, felt slighted by the casual form of her invitation. Spitefully, she joined the festivi-ties only to shrivel the infant's head to ashes by magic. Parvati grieved, and Shiva replaced the lost head with the first avail-able one, that of an elephant sleeping in the nearby forest.

The two myths speak volumes about Hinduism. Hindu wor-shipers chuckle affectionately at Ganesh's improbabilities, but their amusement does not lessen their devotion. Thus does Hinduism combine at a stroke the most earthly of human failings and traits with the most abstract worship. Man's soul is recognized to be the reverse side of his psyche. Hinduism is a creed for people, by people, about people.

Onam, a popular festival of Kerala, commemorates the story of Mahabali, a wise and virtuous king of long ago. Within the kingdom of Mahabali injustice and want were unknown. So perfect was his reign that the divinities grew jealous. What, they asked each other, distinguishes this mortal king from the gods? Was there not danger that his subjects would someday no longer feel it necessary to bring gifts to the temples? For all that could be hoped for on earth was being secured to them by Mahabali.

One day the gods saw that Mahabali was preparing to perform a ritual intended to accomplish the very thing they feared: raising himself to the status of the divine. The barrier between mortal and immortal might be bridgeable, but it was jealously defended by the gods. They decided to send Vishnu to foil the good king's plan.

Eight days before the ceremony was to begin, Vishnu took the form of a young *Brahmin* boy and descended to earth. He appeared before Mahabali, small, meek, respectful, insignificant. Mahabali, to whom no one was too lowly to be excluded from the forms of hospitality, asked the youngster if there were anything he needed. "Whatever you require," said the king courteously, "tell me, and I shall see that you have it."

"All I desire," replied the god-boy, "is some space to perform my *Brahmin*'s *puja*. What I can measure off in three steps will suffice."

"Take your three steps, then," said Mahabali, "and the land they enclose will be yours."

Immediately the wily god began to grow larger and larger. He grew until he towered over the greatest of giants. With his first step he covered the earth. His second step encompassed the heavens. Then Vishnu paused, looked around perplexed and inquired, "Is there any place left for my last step?"

"Oh, Lord," answered Mahabali, by then fully aware of the identity of his guest, "place your foot on my head." Vishnu readily assented, knowing that his weight would push the king down to the underworld. But first he granted Mahabali's prayer that he be allowed to return to earth once a year to see that all was well with his beloved subjects.

Onam celebrates the four-day visit of Mahabali. With him comes the bounty of goodness, namely, the harvest. The joy of his arrival is celebrated with boat races. Graceful serpentlike boats, curved sharply upward at one end, are rowed by a hundred oarsmen apiece. The race is accompanied by the beat of drums and cymbals and the singing of songs. Each boat is hung with golden tassels and scarlet silk umbrellas. The more umbrellas above a boat, the greater the wealth of the family who owns it.

Gods may be cunning, angry, bountiful, fearful, jealous, comforting. Sometimes, though, they are simply playful. Holi is a festival celebrating the games of Krishna, another incarnation of Vishnu, and his milkmaid consort Radha. Fittingly, it is a festival for children.

Color is the stuff of which Holi is made. Children roam the streets smearing each other and all passersby with scarlet, green, shocking pink and royal blue powders. Every house is approached, every occupant decorated. The more boisterous revelers fill plastic squeeze-bottles, specially marketed for the occasion, with colored water and squirt anything squirtable: other children, mothers, fathers, grandparents, aunts, cousins, uncles, pedestrians, cyclists, bullocks, cows, goats, windows, cars, trees, flocks of migrating birds. Nothing can escape.

For every other festival, celebrated by whatever community or religious group, people don their newest, most colorful clothing. For Holi alone are the oldest, most-faded rags pulled from storage bins and worn. Holi, therefore, demolishes the obvious differences between rich and poor. It is a holiday enjoyed equally by prince and by pauper. Hinduism gives to each his chance. Holi is a beggar's day.

Gate of Red Fort, New Delhi

On the road to Kalighat Temple, Calcutta

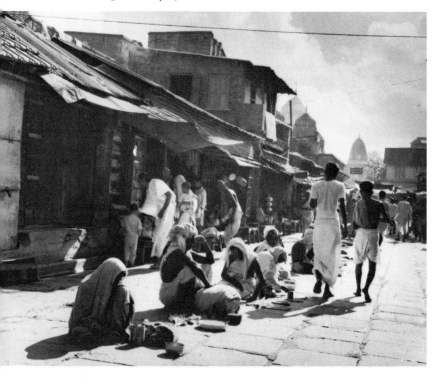

A rickshaw in a Calcutta street on a monsoon day

A fair in Darjeeling

A fair in a Sankal tribal village, Bihar

Women washing utensils in a river in Onissa

A Punjabi housewife in her kitchen in a working-class home

A girl selling vegetables in a Darjeeling m[a]

Workers building a dam, B[

9

Women

GITA, a girl of three, her five-year-old brother, Vikram, and her father are making paper rockets in the sitting room. It is hot. The father becomes thirsty.

"Gita," says he, "run and get me a glass of water."

"For me, too," chimes in Vikram.

Gita never wonders why her father asks that she, not Vikram, bring his water. Gita knows it is because she is a girl.

Ravi is the youngest of five children and the only boy. All his sisters go, or have gone, to school. The older two went to work as soon as they graduated from high school. The next one graduates this year and would like to go to college. But she will not; her father is already searching for a secretarial job for her. The youngest girl attends a free government school nearby. The classes are too large, the teachers overworked and uninterested. But at least the school is in walking distance. There are no transport expenses to be paid.

Ravi is sent to the finest boys' school in the city. His tuition fees are as much as one working sister's salary. Although he is only in third grade, his parents often dream of the day he will enter the university. Ravi feels that his preferred treatment is natural. Nor do his sisters find it unjust.

Maya rests her four-year-old head sleepily against the knee of her mother, Muni. It is night, and the mother is sitting cross-legged before her cow-dung fire, cooking rice by the light of a dim kerosene candle. She is also nursing an infant, washing *dal*, helping her sister-in-law cut potatoes and otherwise hurrying to fix dinner for fourteen people.

From the still, hot courtyard outside come the rising sounds of the men's conversation. Muni's father is visiting. He is talking politics heatedly with his son-in-law and the other men of the family.

"Equality!" proclaims Muni's father. "How can we progress without equality? We must revamp our most basic social relationships."

Little Maya doesn't understand the political words, but she understands perfectly when her grandfather interrupts his speech to call, "Muni, I need some matches. Bring them from the suitcase in my room."

Maya's mother leaves her cooking, puts the baby in Maya's lap, rinses her hands and silently scurries past the men, across the dark courtyard in the direction of her father's room. As she disappears into the blackness, the old man's voice booms through the night, "Revolution! Nothing but thoroughgoing social revolution can save this land from ruin!"

In city or village, a girl knows from the moment of her birth what it is to be a girl. A female is subservient and secondary to a male. Service is a concept utterly absent from the education of a boy. It is central to that of a girl.

Gita's father feels a special tenderness for his daughter. Toward Vikram, on the other hand, he is always sternly authoritarian. Yet Gita is sent to fetch his water, and both children accept that as her natural role.

Muni's father has only daughters. While he has always wished for a son, his girls are all the more precious to him for lack of a boy. He insisted that his daughters marry men who could provide them with the easiest possible lives. Always he has been solicitous about their well-being and comfort. Yet it never occurred to him that he might act upon his demand for equality by fetching his matches himself instead of interrupting Muni's hectic work in the kitchen.

A kindly Indian parent might well protest that his sons and daughters are equal in his regard. Clearly, though, the sons are more equal than the daughters. Girls may be better loved, in the same way that a soft kitten is more petted than a fierce but valuable pedigreed bulldog; yet the mother of boys is somehow thought to be a better mother, the father a more manly man than are the parents of girls. People are heartily congratulated on the birth of a son. But when the baby is a girl, friends ask whether they will try again.

Both the culture and the economics of joint families set a premium on sons. There is no greater reward for a long-suffering woman than to be transformed into a mother-in-law by the marriage of her eldest son. From the time that boy was born, his mother was proud in the expectation that he would someday bring home a bride for her. No less happy was his father, since he knew that the boy would bring his family wealth: both his earnings when he began to work and a dowry, the huge treasure that his bride's family would send along with the girl. Pity the poor father of a girl, though. All he can expect his infant daughter to bring him is expense, expense and more expense. First she must be married, her dowry provided and the wedding celebrated with a pomp far exceeding the family's means, lest their means be belittled in the neighborhood's esteem and their precious prestige suffer. Even after her costly marriage the daughter will be sure to return annually for a visit, bringing with her an ever-increasing horde of hungry grandchildren. However fond a father may be of his daughter, how can he view her as anything but a financial burden?

Yet no father would ever consider not marrying his daughter. Marriage is the proper fate of woman. If a father fails in his task of securing this natural state for his girls, he has failed in a basic religious duty. He is disgraced within his community. Some fathers may also consider the misery their daughters would experience if left unmarried. Childless and therefore denied the prestige of sons and the reward of daughters-in-law, dependent on the charity of father and brothers, the unmarried woman is not even taken seriously enough to be ridiculed or scorned. Worse, she is tolerated. Hindus acquire merit through charity.

Most girls are married, though, and married young. A century ago it happened often that newborn infants were engaged; the wedding was celebrated five or six years later. More common still were brides between the ages of nine and fourteen. By the time a girl was sixteen, she was already being tolerated as a spinster and transformed into a nonperson.

The suitable age for a bride has been a topic of considerable discussion in recent years. Early in this century a law was enacted stating that a bride must be at least fourteen. The minimum age for Hindu girls has since been raised to fifteen. Young though that may sound, many fathers still think fifteen to be horribly old. Rarely, however, do they rant and protest the law. They take instead a more practical course: they ignore it. Although economic pressures have tended to raise the age of boys at marriage, so that they are most often wed when over twenty-five, girls are still very often married between nine and sixteen.

The exceptions are, again, well-off city girls like Seema. Her father and most others of his class agree that it is best to let a girl finish her schooling and go on to the university or work for a while to have a taste of life before marrying. More and more often the urban bride is from two to ten years older than the girl being married in the village.

Child marriage is not the only custom to die hard. Muslims, the second-largest religious community in India, still believe in polygamy. The more wives a man has, the greater his prestige. Today, the law limits the number to four. Poverty often cuts it down to one or two; it is expensive to wed, expensive to keep a wife. But the wish is the same as it always was.

Whatever may be her age, wherever she may live, the chances are still overwhelming that the time for a girl's marriage will be decided not by herself but by her father. More important still, her husband will also be chosen by her parents. The search for a bridegroom is aided by brokers, friends, relatives and classified ads. "Beautiful graduate Brahmin girl wanted for Brahmin engineer earning six hundred rupees a month," reads a typical ad.

Each possibility is carefully interviewed by the father of the bride. First of all, the boy's caste, subcaste and family group must be known; if any one is wrong, the negotiations stop dead. If they are acceptable, then the girl's relatives want to know: How rich is the father-in-law-to-be? How far away does he live, and will the bride live in a joint family? What is the earning power of the boy? How much will he someday inherit? How much dowry will his father demand, and how much can be whittled off the amount by bargaining? How many of the boy's relatives will have to be fed at the wedding feast? If the father is fond enough of his daughter, or if the girl is strong-willed enough, there are other questions: Is this a boy whom my daughter will find compatible? Will my girl be happy as well as well-provided for? These are hard questions to answer. All that can be known about a prospective groom must be based on rumor and impression.

Whatever the difficulties, whatever the cost in pots and pans, jewelry, furniture, clothing and wedding festivities, husbands are ultimately found for most girls. Marriage follows the negotiations quickly, often within a few weeks. Then the bright-eyed, playful village girl suddenly finds herself to be a shy, sari-clad wife, instructed by tradition and her mother-in-law to keep her eyes down and her head covered.

Every marriage, wherever in the world it takes place, marks a major change in the bride's life. Nowhere, though, is that change quite so dramatic as it is in India, and especially in village India. The bride of most other lands is a fairly independent miss. Often she has lived away from her family, in a college dormitory or a career girl's apartment. She knows her husband intimately, sympathizes with his ambitions and his beliefs, wants to share his style of living, has met his relatives. To some degree she has also experimented sexually with him. Married life may be a new adventure, but it is not a dark unknown.

How different is the lot of the young Hindu bride in India! She has probably lived away from her parents' home not more than a week or two of her life, and then only when she visited relatives or attended out-of-town weddings. She has never spoken with her husband and has probably never seen him. The groom and his father may have interviewed her, but if so, she kept her eyes firmly fixed on the floor. She knows no one in her husband's household, probably no one in his village or town. The man she weds could not be more completely a stranger to her.

Comes the wedding day. The bridegroom's party arrives in procession. They are greeted, fed, shown to their quarters. The blare of a brass band—the musicians clad in gold-trimmed uniforms, spats and sandals—mingles with the tom-tom-tom of the *tabla* drums and the noise of bustling festivity. Only the bride is quiet, sitting cross-legged inside the house, tensely detached from the activity.

The order of events and the ceremony itself vary greatly from place to place. In Bengal it all takes four days filled with food and *puja*. The wedding of *Brahmins* in Kerala lasts fifteen minutes. In Delhi the celebrations take up an evening, the ceremony itself about half an hour.

However long the wedding lasts, the bride is handled like a pliant puppet. Draped in a bright red sari embroidered with gold, her feet and hands painted with intricate designs, her head and hair heavy with jewels, her heart thumping with a mixture of excitement and dread, she is led through the rituals. Her little finger is poked into the ears of her in-laws. Her bare feet are placed on certain trays. Her head is anointed with crimson powder, which she will wear thereafter as the sign of her married state. Finally, she is led seven times around a sacred fire with the end of her husband's shawl tied to her submissive neck.

Then it is over, and the bridegroom's party departs. With them goes the bride, alone or, if she is lucky, accompanied by her father or brother. It is a tearful, often hysterical, departure. However much a girl may have enjoyed playing at being a bride, however proud she may have been of the attention and the finery she had suddenly acquired, now she is abruptly plunged back into a far different reality.

That reality is as bittersweet as cooking chocolate. The young bride in her in-laws' house is an outsider, a stranger among people clannishly knit together, or so it seems to her.

At first she is displayed. The in-laws are proud of "their" new wife. Coveys of neighborhood women come to peer into her face, to approve her pretty eyes and condemn her crooked nose, to compare her with other brides in other houses. They finger the fabrics of her saris and speculate on their cost. They weigh the gold of her bangles and necklaces in their palms. They question her minutely about her father's fortune, family and household.

While the worth of this new wife is thus being assessed, her mother-in-law and husband stand by, proud but also anxious. They have, they know, gotten the best bride available under the circumstances. But they also know that those circumstances, their own fortune and standing, are busily being judged by the neighbors who weigh the qualities of the bride.

The forbidding board of neighborly assessors is made up of ordinary women, each of whom has undergone the same ordeal as the young wife now before them. None of them intend to be unkind or pitiless. Yet each is tangled up in her appointed role. These are the Married Women of the Community, and they know of no other way to meet the new addition to their ranks than by scowling at her dull hair and coughing at her pimples.

Nor do the in-laws and the husband find it possible to give much more sympathy. The bridegroom may sense vaguely the pain of separation and the excitement of new adventure that his bride is experiencing as she enters her new world. But he can hardly share her feelings, and certainly he cannot comfort her. In the catalog of husbandly virtues, empathy is missing. All relationships between husband and wife are fixed and formal; all exclude the chance that either may regard the other as human. A wife, for instance, may never pronounce her husband's name. In conversations with others she must always refer to him as "your brother," "your son," "your father," "your son-in-law." How difficult to think of someone else's son or father as a real person when you are forbidden to think of him as Veenu, Rama, Subodh or Amalankar—a man.

Even into sexual intimacy do family compulsions intrude. Remember that the newly married girl has had no chance to experiment with sex. She comes to the bridal bed cold and ignorant. She has never been kissed, has been punished for anything hinting of flirtation. No married sister or wise mother has told her what to expect; the topic is forbidden by custom. Nor is the man by her side an understanding and experienced one; rather is he a fumbling lad, almost as strictly denied the chance to test his sexual confidence as she.

Hanging over the bed of these two frightened innocents, total strangers only a few hours before, is a command writ large by custom: produce a baby before a year is up! A barren bride is scorned and ridiculed. Not even those modern brides who hold loftily to the principles of family planning and insist they want a few years of freedom before having children can escape the doubt and derision of the older women.

Foremost among the promoters of prompt childbearing is the mother-in-law. Her son's wife is her reward for submission and patience. The first duty of the daughter-in-law is to obey her husband's mother. What better way can the mother-in-law flex her newly found muscle of authority than by seeing to it she has a grandchild before her son's first wedding anniversary? The mother-in-law is the vehicle of tradition, and often she believes the best form for that vehicle is the bull-dozer.

Not for nothing does the mother of an unruly girl-child threaten that she will be sent away to her father-in-law's house. The new bride is, for a while, a lonely stranger in a familiar yet fearful land. Gradually, though, she begins to form new friendships. Her husband and mother- and father-in-law may not seem human. With her elder brothers-in-law all communication is forbidden. She may never speak with them, and she must always cover her head and face with her sari in their presence. But her sisters-in-law, especially the wives of her husband's brothers, are girls like herself who have suffered what she does and survived it. Toward them, and toward her younger brothers-in-law, does her heart turn.

The girls of the family conduct her from the fearful bridal chamber, and the even more fearful courtyard where the neighborhood women gather, into the protective womb of the kitchen. Ultimately it is that old friend work that pops the taut bubble of the bride's loneliness. In the kitchen the next twenty years or more of her life will be spent. Here she will find her element, her domain, her field of mastery . . . and her prison.

Very soon she is squatting with the others over the fire, tiny tins of spices and baskets of vegetables spread around, a brass pot of water for cleaning food at one elbow, another with fresh water for the curry next to it. Lithely, with the grace of expertise, she bends and reaches, rarely shifting her heels from their original spot. Five minutes of that squatting position would finish a western woman's back and shoulders for a week. Everywhere in the world flat-footed squatting is natural to a child. But people who are rich in chairs outgrow it, letting their muscles soften and atrophy in the cradle of their furniture. Indians, less affluent in chairs, don't; their squatting muscles always remain limber and functional. And function they do in the kitchens of the land. Even most city women, aside from those of the upper middle class, still continue to cook in the usual way on the concrete floors of their urban flats. The kitchen of a Calcutta middle-class apartment, if there is one at all, is a perfectly bare room with a water tap and drain in one corner.

The duties of the kitchen-bound women are three-fold: to cook; to produce and nurse babies, handing them over to Grandma for any other attention that might interfere with the kitchen work; and to obey husband and elders, especially mother-in-law. Any Hindu will tell you how revered women are in India. Most of the divinities are women. Durga, the mother goddess, is very popular. Why, even cows are worshiped because they symbolize Mother, producer of milk; bringer of abundance, comfort and well-being. Yet, like the cow, the young mother is worshiped with one hand and abused with the other. And like the cow, she is adored as the symbol of plenty and overworked as its practical bearer.

Overworked she remains for many years. But always there lurks one hope: someday she will be a mother-in-law. Produce sons, whispers the older lady, and you shall someday have daughters-in-law. Remain barren—and bearing girls is the same thing—and you shall live the whole of your life in the kitchen.

As she grows older, as the time for her sons' marriages comes nearer, the woman of the kitchen becomes more and more involved in what has hitherto been a secondary but constant part of her life: religion. Her own mother-in-law was always the family priest, the keeper of fasts, the performer of ritual, the conveyor of fables and epic tales. The younger women assisted her as required, but independently they rarely performed *puja* themselves. As her husband's mother becomes senile, however, as she herself finally sees her sons married and their grandmother given over to the funeral flames, the lady of the kitchen becomes once and for all the lady of the temple next door.

Religion is woven through all the strands of an older Hindu woman's life. Every morning she rises with the sun and the hoopoe birds to sprinkle purifying water over the threshold of her house. She next visits field or bathroom, cleans herself with water, scrubs her teeth, and if she is not the most orthodox of upper-caste widows, has a cup of morning tea. Then she finishes her morning tasks: planning the day's meals, selecting vegetables and sending off for fish or meat, measuring rice and *dal*, seeing the younger women started in the kitchen. Now the Hindu mother-in-law is free to embark on the part of the day dearest to her heart. She bathes, preferably immersing herself in a pond or river. She wears her sari and occupies herself for a few minutes with cleaning its free-floating ends. If she is well-off, she may use an old sari to bathe in while she washes the one she has worn since the previous day's bath. In any case, she makes the longest possible job of her bath, luxuriating in the cool water, dawdling over her ritual bows to the east, enjoying every sensual-religious moment of it.

From the bath the dripping woman hurries to change into an off-white handwoven sari that is used exclusively for making *puja*. Then she settles herself for a long spell in her temple. She sets out her goddesses; lights incense; arranges fruits, sweets and flowers; fingers her holy book. Then she pops into the kitchen for a sniff of the curry and an edict that more salt be added. She stoops outside the kitchen door to feed a grandchild his glass of milk or to oil a small head. Finally, she begins the *puja* proper. Depending upon the frequency of interruptions from the cooks and the children, her *puja* may take anywhere from ten minutes to an hour.

Afterward, she changes her sari again, sees the children and men fed, eats her afternoon meal, prepares and chews a delicacy called *pan*—betel leaf filled with nuts and seeds—and lies down for her nap. Late afternoon is visiting time. Neighbors pop in, or the women drift next door for another *pan* and a chat.

Sunset requires another *puja*, after which the implements

and images of the ritual are bedded down for the night. The long evening is spent supervising the kitchen, listening to the men's talk, gossiping with neighbors. The evening meal is a late one. Another *pan,* and it is bedtime. But first the mother-in-law secures her door, bows to the east and sighs loudly her thanks for having seen another day to its end.

Thus does Hindu ritual form the crux of the mother-in-law's life. But it does more. It also provides the escape from routine. Every fall the women of Bengal leave their kitchens, don new silk saris and go off in coveys to view and admire the altars extolling the goddess Durga. Elsewhere in India the divinity most admired by women is Ganesh or Krishna or Lakshmi. But nowhere are women without their special festival. Weddings, infant-naming ceremonies, even funerals, provide women with the chance to escape the dreary sameness of their lives, to wear their exquisite saris and heavy golden marriage jewelry, to travel a bit, rest a bit, meet distant friends and relatives, and gossip a lot. Without the relief of festivals and ceremonies, the rates of feminine insanity would be far, far higher than they are.

But if religion is a Hindu's woman's solace, it also holds for her a bitter threat. Girls are married young, boys old. The chances are therefore good that most women will be widows before they die. For the Hindu widow, religion and custom are terrible tyrants, stripping her life of pleasures and inflicting on her awesome duties and restrictions.

The widow must shave her head, and if she is truly devout, keep it shaved. When her husband dies, she is enjoined to "break her bangles," a ritual made dramatic by the fact that most women wear jingly glass bangles all up and down their forearms. Thenceforth, she may never wear a piece of jewelry. Nor may she wear color, but must go always clad in plain white clothing. She must wipe the customary spot of red from her forehead, and she may never again wear the *bindi*. That spot is, therefore, a sign that a woman is not a widow.

More terrible still are the rules governing diet. These vary from caste to caste, but in general the widow may not eat meat, fish or eggs, onions, garlic, certain high-protein *dals*. Tinku's grandmother, a Bengali *Brahmin* widow, may eat rice only once a day, and that rice must be milled in a special way. For the evening meal she is allowed only fruit, milk and cereals. If she rises from her meal before finishing, she may not continue to eat again. Water, salt, *ghee* and whatever else she may require must therefore all be in reaching distance before she begins, lest she forget and rise to get something for herself. More commonly, a daughter-in-law stays nearby to serve her anything she wants.

For an old woman the life of a widow is difficult and austere. For a young widow it is tragic. A Hindu widow may not remarry. Until a hundred years ago it was thought proper for high-born widows to cremate themselves on the funeral pyre of their husband. That cruel custom of *sati* has been abolished, but the living death of a childless, uneducated young widow may be even worse.

Nilima was married at fifteen to a healthy boy of twenty-five. Her husband was handsome, well-placed, the golden boy of his huge joint family. Quite a match for Nilima, nodded her neighbors approvingly.

Six months after the wedding Nilima watched her young husband, his once strapping body wasted by tuberculosis, being carried out to the funeral fire. Nilima dutifully allowed her thick black locks to be shaved. She broke her bangles with the same docility she had shown when led around the marriage fire six months before. Her huge black eyes dry and blank, she followed her father home to her parents' house. Day after day Nilima sat at home staring into the vacuum of her future, silent, stunned, hopeless.

What Nilima saw before her was a lifetime as the unloved dependent of relatives, without position, without respect, without the promise of sons and daughters-in-law. Her father, his heart breaking for his child, suggested that they defy tradition and find her a second husband. She refused. Quietly she said, "Some evil of mine in another life sent my husband to the pyre before his time. Shall I inflict my fate on yet another man?" Her father enrolled her in a teachers' training institute. He tried instructions in handicrafts, nursing, food-preserving methods. In everything Nilima obediently attended her lessons, but to nothing would she bring the enthusiasm and love that had been cultivated in her since birth to be given to husband and children.

On the young widow Nilima, Hinduism visited everything most cruel. Nilima was unlucky. Lili, on the other hand, is a woman who has had the best possible life offered by Hinduism. Her parents, like Nilima's, spared no effort to find her a husband who would care for her well. Sailen, they felt sure, would do so. The youngest son of a small landowning family, Sailen was a doctor with a lucrative and secure government post in Delhi.

Lili's parents were quite right about Sailen. Lili, sixteen years his junior, became his adored pet. It was his delight to protect her, to tell her of his work, to ask her opinion and advice. Scrupulously, Lili declined to give either; she listened sweetly, clucked when Sailen seemed deserving of sympathy, applauded when he merited praise, laughed when he gaily reported some departmental triumph. Soon they had two sons and two daughters. What more could Lili want of life?

Lili herself was well aware of her good fortune. She was intelligent and perceptive. Yet even when all her children had been well married, when healthy, bright grandchildren had come to storm the old people's sugar tins, Lili had about her a quality that suggested something less than full contentment. Too often she was petulant, almost childlike, incapable of asserting the simplest wish in a straightforward way.

Lili remained so immature because she had never in her life made a decision. She had never had a responsibility that could not be handed on to father, husband or mother-in-law. She had never felt the satisfaction of knowing that she had chosen wisely or acted well. Always dependent on the decision of someone else, Lili had grown old with one part of her personality stillborn.

Why do Hindu women put up with a dependence that would be unbearably irksome to a western or a Chinese woman? Why do marriageable girls and young wives not rebel? For rebel they most clearly do not. A newly married woman may willfully fail to add an extra pinch of salt to the curry after she has nodded acceptance of her mother-in-law's command to do so. But more heady disobedience is rare. Women's liberation and like movements are thought in India to be a joke. The power of western women to limit the number of their children is admired. Otherwise, the ladies of India view their emancipated sisters in other lands more with horror, pity and ridicule than with envy.

The reasons go back to the beginnings of a girl's life. From the moment she is born, she is prepared for her subservient role in life. Her parents may be happy she is a girl. But there is always a hint that they would have been happier had she been a boy. Demands for small services suggest to her that her existence may only be justified through her obedience to elders and to boys. Then comes adolescence: when left to develop naturally she would test herself as a person and as a woman, establish her own integrity and confidence. But she is not left to develop naturally. Instead, the girl is handled like a passive bouquet, bartered over by her father and her bridegroom's family and dispatched from her father's house to a new milieu. There, everyone seems to judge her, not by her basic qualities, but by the size of her eyes and her dowry, both traits over which she has no power.

In fact, she cannot help feeling that she has no power over anything, not even over her own vitality. Early freedoms have developed in her a healthy sensuality. Just as it blooms, she is commanded to wrap it up, to cover her face and legs, to expend her sexual energy exactly where and when its true owners, the men and the elders, decide it should be used. How can a girl believe anything but that she is incapable of handling her own sexuality, or her own self?

Sensing that she cannot control her most potent vitality, she feels it to be a fearsome thing. What if she should disobey her elders without meaning to? Her father or father-in-law might wrathfully cast her out. How could she survive without them? Who then would support and control her?

Soon the fears lead her to mystic regions. Easily ruffled gods and goddesses lurk behind every bush. If she drinks a cup of tea today, a fast day, tomorrow her womb may shrivel. If she nurses her baby where ill-wishing neighbors can see her breast, the evil eye might sour the milk. If she refuses her mother-in-law's order to cook a huge meal on a torrid night when nobody wants to eat it anyway, her husband might die before morning. The specific fear of punishment for rebellion is bad enough. It is intolerable when joined to a thousand vague fears of the supernatural.

The only way a girl can live with herself is by fully accepting the standards of her elders. Indian women can see no reason to rebel. Lili remained immature, but she was never truly dissatisfied. Without dissatisfaction, without the dream of a better lot, how can there be rebellion?

Are there, then, no modern women in India, ladies with careers that have helped to wean them from the pattern of submission? Are they not possible supporters of women's liberation?

India is the land of paradoxes; career women abound. India's medical colleges and graduate schools are full of women. A far higher percentage of doctors are women here than in the United States. Women chemists and lawyers are appearing in increasing numbers. Politics is a favorable field for female activists. Leaders like the poetess Sarojini Naidu and the journalist Aruna Asaf Ali played crucial roles in India's fight for independence.

The most famous Indian woman in politics is Indira Gandhi. When first she became prime minister, capital tongues wagged that she had won the post only because she was the daughter of Jawaharlal Nehru, chief among modern India's founding fathers, who had died a year before. But it didn't take long for Indira Gandhi to prove to the cynics that she held power as nobody's daughter. She was definitely prime minister in her own right, a lady of political skill and steely will.

Indira Gandhi is a true daughter of India. But just as truly is Indian womanhood symbolized by the mute, veiled Hindu bride being led by her husband seven times around the marriage fire. That contradiction is difficult enough to fathom. But at its core lies an even harder one. The highly educated, highly cultured modern woman of India is usually far from being free of traditional social restraints. She may shed her usual work role; she may win world-wide acclaim for her abilities. But within her family she answers almost as readily to authority as does the red-clad bride in the far-off village of Bajitpur. In fact, she is a career woman only by leave of father, husband, mother-in-law.

A young girl was marked by her "advanced and progressive" father to be a scientist. Said the father to his friends, "I believe women should use their brains and be part of the world. My daughter will be a chemist." The girl was a good student, but not a brilliant one. Studiously, obediently, she applied herself and qualified for the science course. Doggedly she crammed her way through the university. Painfully she passed her master's examination in chemistry.

The girl taught for a few years in a secondary school. One day she applied for two weeks' leave, effective the next Monday. The headmistress asked why. "I'm to be married day after tomorrow," said the teacher. Her father had found a well-off businessman who wanted a scientist wife, and after the usual formal interview, the chemist had been betrothed to him.

After the wedding the bride taught another year, then quit to have her first baby. While she was still unemployed, and while her husband was abroad on a business trip, a friend, the owner of a travel agency, asked her to work for him temporarily. She obliged and found, to her delight, that she enjoyed the work. Never had she looked forward to going to school, college or job. Now each day was a challenge and satisfaction. When her husband returned, she asked his permission to continue at the agency.

"Absolutely not!" declared he. "I married a chemist, and you shall remain a chemist." He arranged a post for her in a commercial laboratory, and there she still works, dreamy-eyed, bored, submissive.

Another lady careerist is a lawyer and a leader of her profession. Few advocates are honored with permission to argue before the Supreme Court; she is one of them. She is the author of a learned book on divorce law, her specialty. She is chairman of a national women's organization and of the association of women lawyers. Unmarried, she lives with her mother, brothers, sisters-in-law, nieces and nephews in a typical joint family. She is roundly scolded by her mother if she comes home later than ten o'clock at night. Once she tried to move away; her mother forbade it; she stayed.

Dress is one indication of how little liberated the women of India are. Early in this century a profound revolution shook the foundations of Chinese society. Educated women were in the forefront of the modernization that resulted. At the same time that they overthrew the authority of their elders and their menfolk, the New Age girls cut their long locks, unbound their feet and discarded their traditional Chinese costumes for the practical skirts of the West. Almost every other nation of the world has seen its women do likewise. However much grace and variety may have been lost as a result, the movement toward short, simple, easily cared for costumes is part of the feminine urge toward freedom.

Indian women have yet to make that move. Even when they live in other lands, they take their saris with them and wear them not simply for ceremonial occasions but always. Short hairstyles have a limited popularity in New Delhi and Bombay. Elsewhere a woman whose hair is cut is apt to be a widow. New Delhi girls like bell-bottom pants worn with *kurtas*. But so close is the costume to the more traditional *churidar* and *kurta*, tight-fitting pants puckered at the ankles and loose-fitting hip-length top, that the step is a tiny one. Most Indian girls, from the time they reach marriageable age, cannot bring themselves to bare their legs. Trousers are tolerable to the most advanced. Skirts are a declaration of sexual independence many degrees more radical than India's women are yet willing to make.

Almost everywhere the sari is still the garment of most classes of women, although in every region the women have their own distinctive style of wearing it. A sari is simply six yards of unstitched fabric tucked, folded and draped around a body-hugging blouse and an ankle-length petticoat. It can be wrapped round and round until the woman's figure is hidden in a mountain of material. It can also be smartly pleated in front, pulled snugly around the hips and tucked over the bodice in a way that accents every curve. The style of the sari is one milestone indicating the distance its wearer has traveled along the road to modernity. But whether fashionably tight or modestly loose, it is still a sari: elegant, graceful, sweeping, confining, old-fashioned.

More revealing still of its wearer's position is the *purdah* donned by Muslim women. *Purdah* means literally "curtain"; it refers to the custom of keeping women in isolation, shut off from the public parts of a house, behind a curtain. Women in *purdah*, on the occasions when they do venture out-of-doors, take their curtains with them. The *purdah* they wear is a robe, black or brown or white. It starts at the top of the head and ends at the ankles. Over the face is either a small gauze-covered box or a veil through which the lady can see but not be seen. Underneath the robe is the same gay, alive, brilliant sari worn by women free of *purdah*. Women in *purdah* are literally the possessions of their menfolk. They may not be touched, befriended, spoken to, or even seen, by any other male.

Purdah was once customary for upper-class Hindus as well as for Muslims. Now it is confined to Muslims, who introduced it to India six centuries ago. Hindu women have gone back to the relative freedom of an earlier day.

But even some Muslim girls today take liberties with their *purdah*. Walk behind these girls and you will think them to be discreetly draped in the usual way. But when you pass them and look back, you will have a surprise. Their robes are teasingly unfastened in front. Gay saris or stylish *kurtas* flare enticingly out from underneath. The head veils are thrown rakishly up to reveal giggling, lipsticked mouths in pretty, frank faces framed by stylish hairdos. The modern vitality of these girls plays peek-a-boo with their traditional fetters.

Laughing charm glimpsed beneath a veil that is parted but not discarded: here is the paradox of Indian womanhood in a single image.

10

Play Spans the Ages

"KABADI KABADI KABADI KABADI," chant the children of Bajitpur as Tinku runs furiously after a squealing, barefoot girl. Are these some strange and exotic rites? No, the youngsters are merely playing tag.

In thousands of lands, wherever children romp, tag is one of the games enjoyed. If Seema, child of urban Delhi, were to visit Tinku in his village, almost everything would be as strange to her as to a child from Alaska or France. But Seema, the Alaskan and the Frenchman would all be able to join Tinku in a game of *kabadi* after a mere moment's observation.

Nor would tag be the only game those otherwise diverse children could share. So much of play is common, in fact, that it is the natural bridge on which children with different languages, different dress, different manners, can meet to make friends. Play spans the distance and the ages separating almost any two points in the world.

Girls everywhere make mud cakes, although in India they are mud *roti*. Everywhere they jump rope, dress up in their mother's clothes and play hopscotch.

There are, of course, other games unique to an area. Small girls in Bajitpur, for instance, play a game called *kattal khela*, which could only have developed in a land where *kattal*, or jackfruit, grows. *Kattal* is a large thorny fruit, prized also as a vegetable when it is unripe. It is cut into tiny cubes and curried with potatoes and sharp spices. A delicacy with a very short season, it cannot be preserved. Nor can it ordinarily be enjoyed in very large amounts even when it is available, for its preparation is tedious and time-consuming. The flesh is surrounded by a sticky pulp that glues the cook's fingers together and exasperates all efforts at efficiency. Young mouths water all the more freely for *kattal* curry because mothers so often answer demands for it with, "Maybe tomorrow. I haven't the time today."

Kattal khela comes from the love children have for this favored fruit. One small girl stands with her arms raised; she is the *kattal* tree. Several others grab her arms and shoulders; they are the *kattal* hanging from the tree. One girl is selected by matching fingers to be the *mali*, or gardener, who tends the tree. Each of the remaining children comes in turn to buy a *kattal*, offering the *mali* in payment the "coin" of a stone, a leaf, a twig. The *mali* becomes finicky, refusing some coins, accepting others. When a sale is concluded, the buyer pulls one *kattal* from the tree. Often she must tug mightily. This Bengali answer to The Farmer in the Dell continues until each customer has found acceptable money and each *kattal* has been plucked.

Kattal khela is usually played by little girls, but not always. The tree may be male and nine years old, the *mali* his three-year-old sister. The shoppers and *kattals* may range in age from minus-two to over-ten. Playmates in India are rarely all of the same age and sex. Younger ones invite older children to join their games, and the big ones do so with all the verve, laughter and interest of the babies. Often big children will invent special games just so tiny playmates can join in. Nobody suffers for the mixing of ages; nobody resents it.

Bicycle racing in Delhi is a good example. If there are many onlookers too young to cycle, the riders will handicap themselves by adding infant bulk. The winner of one race takes on his handlebars the largest of the babies for the next. Adults may scream of dangers, but the children—riders and passengers—are joyfully content. If the parents insist that the risks are too great, the whole gang may take to tricycles instead. A girl of twelve streaks gleefully down the road, her long legs working clumsily at the small pedals, while a three-year-old boy bends expertly over his handlebars and dashes ahead to the finish line.

Thus, there is no friction over "taking little brother along." Little brother joins naturally in play with older children, who just as naturally include him in their games.

Ball games are popular in India, the favorite being cricket. It is a cult, followed as baseball is in the United States and Japan. Players are worshiped, games followed on the front pages of daily newspapers, scoring records reeled off by fans in endless discussions of the subject. The game itself, in fact, resembles baseball. A small hard ball is batted with a wide flat bat handled something like a golf club. Instead of running bases, the players dash between two sets of wickets, rows of sticks planted vertically in the ground. Two teams play, each composed of eleven players. But boys find ways of playing casually with fewer people, taking turns pitching, batting and fielding in rotation. Those too young to play retrieve long hits and fouls.

At times the passion for cricket gives way to football, or soccer, as it is called in the United States. Most boys' games in

Indian cities are very similar to those of boys in the West. A European or American boy would whistle admiringly at the collection of *gutti,* or marbles, of a boy in Calcutta or Madras. They would all share an enthusiasm for flying kites and spinning tops.

Ingenious young villagers make up for a lack of toys by using instead materials abundantly at hand. *Phoottka khela,* for instance, requires nothing more than mud, practice and patience. A ball is fashioned from mud or, less often, from wheat dough. The ball is flattened between the palms to make a disk, which is then turned and pressed with the fingers until it is shaped into a bowl. The bowl is then turned upside-down and thrown sharply to the ground, whereupon it pops, hopefully with a resounding bang. Competitions are held; children take turns adding clay or dough to the same ball, each one trying to outdo the explosion of the others. Don't underestimate the degree of skill this game requires. The rim of the bowl must be perfectly even, the throw precise, to produce any sound at all. A mere squeak is as good as a miss.

Phoottka khela is played by both girls and boys, but only in villages. *Goolidanda* is a boys' game, and it is equally well loved in city and country. *Goolidanda* is a kind of tiddlywinks with sticks. Two sticks, a long one and a short one, both tapered at the ends, are used. The player holds the long stick and with it strikes the end of the short one as it lies on the ground. The small stick thereupon flies up into the air. Then the boy wields the long stick again, this time as a bat to send the small one flying as far away as possible. The distances achieved are measured, and the boy who sends the stick farthest is the champion. Tinku and his neighbors in Bajitpur play *goolidanda* with twigs found beneath the mango trees. Lucky, Seema's brother, has a beautifully fashioned pair of sticks made of solid teakwood and painted with bands of color. Both Lucky and Tinku play *goolidanda* with the same rules, in the same way.

Unlike *goolidanda, kattal khela* and *phoottka khela,* much of the play of India abides by no rules. Here as everywhere in the world a child's imagination is his brightest toy. That is as true for Tinku as it is for Seema. But it is also true that the differences between Seema's play style and Tinku's are most clearly apparent in their games of fantasy. No human being can create something, not even a half hour's recreation, without drawing on the pools of his experience. The experiences of Tinku and of Seema are as disparate as those of any two humans on earth.

Tinku knows his village, the fields surrounding it, the market town three miles away (which looks like a slightly glorified Bajitpur) and the lore of his own family. He can dream of the monkey-god Hanuman flying on the wind over the seas, for his grandmother has spun that tale from the epic *Ramayana.* But beyond the range of his own small vision and the reach of his grandmother's religious stories, Tinku's stock of experience does not go.

Seema reads the Sunday features in her father's newspaper. She knows about fabulous temples in Cambodia, monorails in Tokyo, great experiments in clearing farmland in the Soviet Union, sky-tickling office buildings in New York. Her neighbors have a television set. During the three hours of evening viewing, Seema sees films of men walking on the moon, documentaries showing microorganisms squirming through vast water-drops, science fiction fantasies of men who live on the ocean bottom. In school she learns of Africa and Japan. Children of diplomats living in the neighborhood tell her of Germany, America and Indonesia. She reads library books and magazines about England, China and Russia. At the movies she glimpses the lives of the very wealthy and the very poor of every land. All this rich stock of experience is hers without her even knowing it. While Tinku's eye of fantasy stops at the line of trees bounding his village and at the end of the *Ramayana,* Seema draws on a wide knowledge of places, people and doings of which the village child can know nothing.

But however vast the airy fields in which Seema's imagination may roam, it starts from precisely the same touchstone as does Tinku's. For both, home base is the rich ritual of Hinduism. Worship involves magnificently festooned gods and goddesses, ceremonies involving fruits and sweets, pungent-smelling incense and colorful flowers. Small wonder that such sense-caressing rituals should animate the imaginations of Hindu children.

But where the villager's play both begins and ends within the religious corral, the city child's roams over vast and often incongruously distant fields. Seema and her friends, for instance, once fashioned a religious altar from a pile of bricks and then made a community talent show from their religious play.

It began one afternoon when the neighborhood children discovered a forgotten pile of bricks in a park near Seema's house. Building at random, they produced a platform that reminded them of the *pandal,* in which *puja* is performed. *Puja* suggests flowers, fruits and incense, so the children ran to their homes to see what they could glean. They returned with a motley collection of bananas and apples. One girl begged her mother for a stick of incense, while Seema organized the younger children to search for flowers in the gardens of the area. As each offering arrived, Seema arranged the *pandal* prettily and then rearranged it to make room for the next. Limp sunflowers and stringy weed-blossoms formed a border; the incense stood mounted in earth at one side; the bananas and apples lay on the bricks. But all the puttering Seema did could not fill the central place, where the images of divinities should have stood. Homeward dashed the children again, returning with mama dolls, teddy bears, miniskirted figurines, red-clad bridal effigies: these became the gods and goddesses.

By then evening had fallen, and the older sisters and brothers of the children strolled into the park. Seema urged the big sister of her friend to sing some *kirtan*, the captivating religious chants that are as much at home in the playground as in the temple. The girl's clear, calm voice beat rhythmically across the park. More strollers gathered around the *pandal*. The single voice gradually swelled to a chorus. When the chant rolled into silence, another girl slipped easily into a popular ditty from a movie. Again other voices joined the chorus. Soon five people offered to fill the silence after each song. A teen-aged boy brought out his guitar, and a girl fetched her *sitar*, the plaintive classical Indian instrument. A nursery school tot pitched in with "Jack and Jill Went up a Hill," and half-a-dozen others followed quickly with other nursery rhymes. Two sisters had meanwhile changed into costumes and danced a rollicking Rajasthani folk-dance. Parents came to call their youngsters home to dinner and stayed to listen, clap and sing. Nobody noticed when the incense burned away. Nobody noticed when the fruit was eaten. Nobody remembered that a mock altar had begun the show.

In the villages it is not the ordinary ritual of daily *puja* that excites the special enthusiasm of children so much as the spectacular occasion of a wedding. The traveling of otherwise village-bound relatives, the music and abundant food, the brilliantly colored clothing and the sparkle of golden marriage-jewelry easily capture the imaginations of youngsters accustomed to the routine of farm life.

Not that life on the land is poor in food for the imagination of a child. Seasons change dramatically, crops grow from nothing to waving seas of green and gold, trees bear fruit and flowers bloom, cows calve and goats bear twins. *Kattal khela* is only one of many games spawned by the abundance of nature. But nature is as familiar to the children of the village as electricity is to a city child. It is not that miraculous glow from a vacuum that inspires Seema to fantasy, but the moon walk of a strangely clad astronaut. Tinku knows of no astronauts. Brides take their place.

Aside from newborn infants, who arrive with such regularity as to be uninteresting, brides are the only village people who come from distant places, the only people from a village who journey to live in new lands. The groom who comes to claim his wife is accompanied by a lively party of gay people. Ordinary in their own village, they are endowed with magic when they descend upon Bajitpur for the four-day festival of marriage. A Bajitpur boy, an ordinary cousin before, is suddenly a knight on a wondrous mission when he departs, with blowing of conch shells and ceremonial cheers, to wed a bride from another village.

It is not surprising that the favorite game of make-believe in Bajitpur and many other villages is the creation of a mock wedding. Dolls are made from clay and colorful bits of rags. Their faces are carefully painted with spices and berry juice; their palms and feet are smeared with vermilion. A room is built from mud, stones and twigs. The ceremonies begin: the dressing of the bride, the arrival of the groom's party, the feasts and rituals of the wedding itself, the departure of the bride for her father-in-law's house. For four days the game continues. Neighbors are fed token sweets, or if the family of the children is very poor, water and bananas. Drums are beaten and *kirtan* chanted.

Though both begin with religious ceremonies, this mock wedding and Seema's *puja pandal* are really very different sorts

of play. The village children's game is carefully planned with
the help of the household's women. Nothing about it is spon-
taneous; it grows not from a chance association but from an
intentional suggestion. Moreover, the village mock-wedding is
rigorously governed by the real rules of marriages. Seema and
her friends, on the contrary, began with a religious ceremony
and ended with a talent show. Their wandering invention
might have turned the *pandal* into a schoolroom, a hospital
ward, a movie star's banquet hall or the control center for a
space flight. But when Tinku and his friends begin a mock
wedding, there is no doubt that four days later a mock bride
will depart, amidst ritual cheers and chants, for her mock
father-in-law's house. The same game has been played in the
same way by village children for as long as Hindu marriage-
rites have been established: a long, long time.

In only one domain does the imagination of Tinku rival
that of Seema. It is a rare city-child who can dream up as
much mischief as a villager. Orchards and livestock offer much
more opportunity to the rural lad than the city child ever has
at hand; further, the casualness of joint family life threatens
much less punishment.

City or country, the natural place to seek a boy during the
fruit season is up a tree—anybody's tree. Mangos, guavas and
small sour fruits called *kul* or *bair* are favorites. In the city an
estate owner who carefully cultivates fruit trees learns to be
sorry he has chosen that pastime. One Calcutta doctor with a
garden full of guava trees became so weary of chasing away
youthful fruit-pickers that he ordered all his trees chopped
down. In a good mango year at Bajitpur Tinku's family calculates the yield less 10 per cent to allow for "fruit eaten in
the tree."

Mischief is not always so functional, but it is rarely intentionally cruel to other people, either. A cripple, for instance,

may be ridiculed behind his back, but he is not openly taunted. City urchins, so abundant in every metropolis and town of India, may snatch a tomato from a vendor's basket or shout "Good Mor-r-r-rning!" saucily at a foreigner. But there is little hatefulness in such fun. Given a jocular answer (such as, "Good morning at six o'clock in the evening?"), these children are ready to laugh with friendly camaraderie. Even among themselves their fierce rough-and-tumble play—and there is no fiercer to be found anywhere in the world—is far more apt to produce boisterous laughter, however pained, than tears.

If humans are not the object of cruelty, animals certainly are. Hinduism holds animals to be sacred. The cow in particular is revered as a central deity. That does not prevent people from throwing stones at her, twisting her tail, playing tag with her terrified calf, beating her eyes and otherwise misusing her.

Nor are sacred cattle the only animals brutalized. Children in Delhi are brought up to be afraid of animals. They run screaming from dogs that are simply strolling peacefully through the streets. Pet dogs are plentiful in Delhi. They are treated with a rude alternation of cuffs and affection. Neighborhood children refuse to enter a friend's house unless the dog is tied up. The young masters are themselves fearful around other people's pets. Let a child of New Delhi be safely entrenched behind a wall or a gate, and he will torment with a storm of stones and sticks the same dog from which he cravenly runs away in open ground. Any smaller animal is fair game for more aggressive bullying. Cats are favorite victims of raucous chases; once cornered, they must endure hilarious tail-pulling and rib-poking until they can again escape.

Village people live with animals on a far more tolerant plane. Dogs, cats, goats, cows, chickens, ducks, pigs, and in some areas camels, elephants and horses are all a natural part of the surroundings and are treated as such. People who are better-off save a handful of rice for the dogs, and house cats are invited to clear the dishes after meals. Nonetheless, gentleness is not the keynote of the villager's attitude toward his livestock. Street curs are kicked out of the way; cats are warded off from the kitchen during mealtime with accurately wielded bamboo sticks; bullocks are prodded, beaten and poked into work. Children delight in chasing baby goats. In their distress the kids cannot decide which way to run and stand bleating futilely until a whack on the rump speeds them in one direction or another. Whether the victim be urban cat or rural kid, the animals of India are treated less than humanely by the humans of the land.

It is easy to condemn such brutality to animals; only a little more difficult to understand it. The most obvious reason is the force of imitation. A child watches an adult chase a cow away from his vegetable garden with a vicious shower of stones, urge his horse to speed with a heavy stick, remove a hungry puppy from his path with the toe of his shoe. Not unnaturally, the child behaves in like style when next he has dealings with a beast. Yet simple imitation is far from being the sole reason.

Brutality hangs in the atmosphere of India like smog in the air of industrial America. It is less the brutality of one human being toward another than that of life toward all. For the poor, be they in town or village, the ferocity of life takes the tangible form of poverty. Paradoxically, the hatefulness of poverty often coexists with love, particularly that of parents for children. Yet that love, for a small hungry child, can only accentuate the cruelty of his fate.

Any baby feels that he is the center of the universe. If he is hungry, his belly is the center of himself. To the child in need of food, Mother means provision; that is especially true when most of an infant's sustenance is sucked from his mother's breast. What happens, then, when the breast is dry because the mother has not eaten enough to produce milk? What happens when the family has nothing else to give the child instead? The baby wails and kicks, complaining not only of the pain in his empty stomach but also of the cruelty of the mother who has, so far as his egocentric view of the world permits him to understand, deprived him of his food. Baby and his hunger come first. Mother exists in order to give. If she doesn't, is not she, and thus the world she represents, cruel and capricious? So feels the inarticulate infant.

As he grows up, the child may learn about wealth and poverty. He may come to understand that some people eat while others go hungry because of fate, injustice, the will of God or some other reason. But intuitively he continues to react toward the world in the way he learned at his mother's flaccid breast. Watch out! warns the memory of that first disappointment. The world may seem kind, but it is not. When you can do so without fear of punishment, strike before you are struck. Roughhousing represents one easy avenue for acting on that philosophy, cruelty to animals another. A kick at a skinny, half-starved cur is a kick at the world of hunger.

Why, though, should a well-fed, well-cared-for New Delhi child like Seema stone a dog? Seema suffers from the opposite complaint of the hungry child: she is too well cared for. Not hunger or cold but manners afflict her. At home she is warned continually not to touch, not to break, not to soil. She is warned to address each "Auntie" and "Uncle" politely and correctly. She is sent at the age of two and a half or three to a nursery school where play is "nicely" planned and controlled. She is sent home with neatly ruled notebooks in which she must write her ABCs fifty times, and her mother insists that she do so before she may play. Wherever rules do not intrude, fears lurk instead. Parents and teachers are forever cautioning her to be careful, not to climb too high on the jungle gym, not to touch an electric wire even if it *is* unplugged, not to go too near the stairs, not to wade in a fresh muddy puddle lest there be a snake in it. The young well-to-do city child thus learns that everything is dangerous. To her, as her infant universe revolves around "I," that means that everything is intent on harming her. Is it so curious that she learns to fear indiscriminately? The pet puppy of her neighbor threatens her; the beggar at her door threatens her; the children with whom she plays threaten her. Hers is an ungentle world, as brutal in her fantasy as is the world of hunger for the poor child in reality. Like the child of poverty, she too learns to return tit for tat.

Cruelty to animals is only one of the forms that return takes. Another is incessant teasing. Younger children may be accepted easily into the games of their elders, but the price they pay is to be teased mercilessly. In the guise of play the big boys and girls pinch the cheeks of the younger ones, tear toys from their hands and pretend to hide them, offer juicy guavas and mangos only to snatch them away again. Teasing is an accepted mode of behavior; adults stand by and laugh at the joke instead of reprimanding the offender.

Generosity and hostility are thus freely mixed in the play of Indian children. Where are they not? In any individual case, the mixture may contain more of one or the other. But in all cases, play is a universal language, a language that says much.

11

School

FOUR BOYS sit cross-legged on the veranda of a box-like brick house in a small Indian town. Around them are scattered brown-paper-covered books, notebooks, slates, pens, ink bottles, pencils and erasers. They are studying.

Whether they are learning is another question. All of them are reading aloud from books. No two of them read the same words or even the same books. Each of them seeks to drown out with his monotone stream of words the voices of the others; the total volume thus steadily increases, although the inflection does not.

Here we have a motorcar it is a carriage on four wheels there is an engine in front it is filled with petrol . . .

. . . Central Africa where the river Congo flows this part of Africa is a big tableland and has a thick forest all over it the trees here grow so close together that there is not much land to till or to build houses in . . .

Akbar was very wise he knew that India was the land of the Hindus so he made friends with them he married Rajput princesses . . .

Play may be an uncharted land to the children of India, one where they may discover new games, create new fantasies. The path of education, though, is littered with very explicit signposts: Read this as if chanting a charm. Write this even if you don't understand. Wear your uniform to school. Stand when Teacher enters the room. Memorize the Correct Answers to questions. Above all, pass The Exam.

The Exam is the end-all of Indian schooling. Coming after ten years in some places, eleven years in others, it shapes all the days, all the minutes, in the schoolroom from Class One onward. It is state-administered, something like the Regents Exam in New York. But unlike other quizzes, which cover a year or two, at most four, of work, the graduation examination in India includes all the work the children have covered in all their school years.

Though The Exam is the same throughout each state, the style of education varies greatly from the one-room village primary school to the multistoried high-tuition education factories filled with the children of the rich in Delhi, Bombay, Madras and Calcutta. The village child marches barefoot to school early in the morning, a slate under his arm and a paddle-like implement printed with the vernacular alphabet and numbers dangling from his hand. Of books he has none. Notebooks are a rare extravagance. Even pen and ink are kept for the important occasions of examinations only.

In school the child sits on a long bench, crammed elbow-to-elbow with several dozen other students of assorted sizes and ages. The teacher, with perhaps fifty or more pupils in his tin-roofed classroom, marches back and forth in the front, shouts a few commands, beats time rhythmically against his thigh with the stout stick he clutches in his hand, yawns, looks conspicuously at his wristwatch if he is fortunate enough to have one, and does nothing enthusiastically except to dismiss class after an hour's ordeal.

Occasionally, a more ardent teacher happens to find his or her way to a village school. Bajitpur has one, a young woman named Sulekha. With fine determination she tries to teach her students at least the basics of reading and writing. Few of them learn. The obstacles are very tall and very wide.

"First of all," complains Schoolmistress Sulekha, "they only come about half the time. Either they are needed at home or else they are ill with dysentery or fever." Malaria has been eradicated from the village, but other fevers abound. The only drinking water available is highly polluted with disease-producing bacteria. Illness is a mighty barricade on the road to education.

"Then," Sulekha continues, "nobody at home encourages them. People don't see the necessity of learning to read. There's nothing *to* read. Once, the landlords' sons here organized a library. But termites and worms ate the books."

Newspapers come rarely, and then only to the well-to-do who can afford to subscribe to them. An occasional order from the government; now and then a postcard from a distant relative written by a professional letter-writer; an infrequent announcement of a wedding about to take place; once in five years, at electiontime, posters and flyers boosting the candidates: these are all the ordinary farmer ever finds to read. Why spend the time and energy to learn a complicated skill like reading when one will make use of it so rarely? Better to remain a part of the crowd of illiterates who press around the village schoolmaster or landlord to hear him read aloud the order or the election pamphlet.

For poor city children, reading matter is more abundant, but the obstacles to literacy are almost as great as they are for villagers. Education is compulsory in the cities, but government-run free schools are scarce. Not everyone can go to them. Even those who do gain admission to a free school find themselves expected to learn under conditions not very much better than those in the one-room village school.

The best of the private schools are very much better than the government schools. High fees eliminate them, though, as possibilities for any but the children of wealthy parents. Often, tuition for one child is as much as the entire salary of a hard-working father of six.

In these schools formality is the rule. Uniforms are required. Girls and boys attend separate schools. Coeducation is an experiment that has not yet appeared on the Indian horizon. A few schools do admit students of both sexes—and then isolate them in separate classrooms.

"Good morning, miss," chant the high school girls in unison as they rise to greet the teacher when she enters the room. The schoolmistress returns their greeting formally, deposits an enormous stack of notebooks on her table, and directs the proctors to pass out these classwork books while collecting the homework ones. She then writes on the board the assignment of classwork: Read pages 26 through 28, and answer questions 1–5 on page 29. While the children do so, the teacher corrects the homework assignment; that is, she makes large red X's beside each "wrong" answer. She must finish quickly before the period ends, so that the notebooks will be available that night for the next assignment. Even if she wants to comment on errors, she has no time to do so. A few minutes before the bell rings, the notebooks are again exchanged between students and teacher. If she has found several common errors in the homework, she may demonstrate or discuss the work. Or she may spend a few minutes introducing new material. Rare is the teacher who leads her students in a discussion. Even rarer is the one who departs from the state-directed syllabus.

So scant is the assistance of the teacher that students must rely heavily on their books. Yet they, too, are of little help. Poorly printed, chock-full of mistakes, they are generally designed to "cover the syllabus" rather than to teach. Nowadays some schools are experimenting with more interesting, colorful, up-to-date texts. The sciences especially are benefiting from the use of new methods. Richly endowed schools often invest large sums in their laboratories, which are sometimes better equipped and designed than the standard undergraduate labs of American universities. But so long as the curriculum is rigidly standardized by the state, departures must be slight. And the curriculum continues to be standardized because The Exam is.

It is The Exam, then, that haunts the life of a city student for ten or eleven years. However good a child's classroom work may have been, failure in The Exam means no diploma. The villager who makes it to the point of graduation usually lives deep in the shadow of The Exam only for a year or two before. For those months he is withdrawn from every form of recreation and plied with books, tutors and prayers in preparation for the awful week. Rich urban private-school student and destitute villager, both spend the final days of preparation pacing their rooms memorizing "correct" answers, which appear in the published texts of old exams. All questions are essay style and all answers are lengthy. An examinee therefore crams his head with hundreds of thousands of words in the hope that enough of the questions whose answers he has memorized will appear on The Exam to give him a passing mark. He knows well that repeating a published answer word for word will not count against him. In fact, the examiner marking papers who recognizes a standard answer correctly written, every *i* dotted every comma in place, will be favorably impressed because the student has memorized so well. It is not surprising, then, that all schooling concentrates on developing the ability to memorize huge chunks of undigested material. Rote is the ideal; original thought is frowned upon. Who knows whether the examiner will recognize an *original* correct answer as being correct?

About all a student is qualified to do once he has passed The Exam is to tick off on his fingers the names of the subjects he has covered: arithmetic, geometry, algebra, history, social studies, home economics for girls (including needlework), general science in the elementary grades. In the last three years each student chooses between humanities and sciences. It is a momentous decision for a thirteen-year-old to make. If he opts for humanities, he may never at any later stage change over to the sciences.

Passing marks on The Exam qualify the student to enroll in the university. There he meets a system identical to the one he has just left. Again he must make an irrevocable commitment to a certain subject. Again the material he reads is standardized and petrified by state curricula. Again he has only badly written textbooks. And again over all his work looms the specter of the examination he must pass to win his B.A. or M.A. degree.

But by the time they reach college, most students wish for nothing more than this robot system. Initiative, curiosity and natural intelligence have long since been stifled. Years of rote learning alone would have done this to most. But those virile brains that might have escaped stultification are further saddled with the monster problem of language.

India is a union of eighteen states, and almost every one has its own language. Fifteen native languages plus English are officially recognized by the constitution, for each is spoken by too many millions of people to be slighted. Each of these is a distinct language, as different from the others as the languages of Europe are from one another. And just as the European tongues are related to one another in overriding families, so within the Indian languages two major groupings exist. Hindi, Urdu, Bengali, Assamese, Oriya and most of the other tongues of north India form one family. The languages of the south, Tamil, Kannada and so on, form another. Kashmiri, the language of the far northwestern mountain-state, sounds more like the central Asian tongues of the Soviet Union than like any other Indian language; it stands outside the two family-groupings. In addition to the official sixteen, there are about one hundred and sixty minor languages spoken by smaller communities all over India. Interwoven with these are hundreds of dialects and regional variations.

When Great Britain conquered India, the foreign rulers realized they must depend on local administrators. So vast was the land, so mammoth the number of bureaucrats needed to man the government posts, that Englishmen alone could never meet the demand. They therefore organized a system of education aimed at developing nothing more nor less than literate clerks. All college classes were taught in English from English texts. In many urban primary and secondary schools as well English was the only language used. Elsewhere English was taught from Class Three onward. This system still continues in most places, despite efforts by independent India to change it.

Language has been one of the most heated issues in the land since it separated from the British in 1947. Everyone recognized very early that one language must be given dominance if India were ever to be more than a loose confederation of separate states. Which language that should be was a moot question. English was disliked for two major reasons: first, it reminded free Indians too sharply of their unfree past; second, and more important, if the whole land were to become literate, if the seventeen out of every twenty people who could not read and write were to be taught, the language of instruction had to be a familiar one. To expect villagers to learn to read a tongue they could not understand was utterly unrealistic. They must obviously become literate in their mother tongue. The official language would have to be one that was known to most people in the land.

That language was Hindi. Not only was it spoken by millions throughout the northern plains, but it was also closely enough related to the languages of millions of others that it could easily be learned by them. To be sure, south Indians would be inconvenienced. For them, Hindi was as foreign a tongue as English. But someone would have to suffer; the choice of Hindi seemed to minimize the number who must.

A plan was accordingly drawn up. English would remain the language of government business for fifteen years. During that time Hindi would be taught widely, and books and forms would be translated. After a decade and a half the switchover would be made. Even then, the regional languages would continue to be important within each state and would be the medium of instruction in most schools. But Hindi would override them all for official purposes.

The plan seemed to make the best of a bad problem. Unfortunately, the people of the south did not think so. Tamil-speaking Madrasis led the opposition, demanding that their own tongue be accorded a position at least equal in importance to that of Hindi. At the end of fifteen years the opposition boiled up into passionate anti-Hindi campaigns and riots. Moreover, the government had done little toward teaching Hindi or translating materials into it. The changeover was postponed. Today, English is still the official language of India.

Some progress has been made. More education is in the

vernacular. More and more government forms and publications are in Hindi. But for the student in an English medium school, the problem is just what it was in British days. In kindergarten he learns English by writing his ABCs and repeating rote sentences over and over again in unison with the rest of his class. He hears nothing but English spoken in most classes. If he wants to understand what his teachers say, he must first understand the language, then the content. Nor is he free to concentrate only on English. He also learns Hindi, for it is still the coming language of the land. If Hindi is not his mother tongue, he learns the latter as well. And most schools also require Sanskrit, a dead language in which the ancient texts of India are written.

School is a burdensome albatross round the neck of the serious scholar in India. Fortunately or otherwise, serious scholars are few. Even today fewer than two out of a hundred youths attend universities. At least two out of every ten children never go to school at all. Most of the other eight attend the sort of one-room classroom we have glimpsed in Bajitpur. Literacy rates have improved over the decades of independence. The quality of education has not. The shadow of the bullock cart still looms much larger on the classroom wall than the speeding shade of the motorbike.

12

To Office on a Motorbike

PICK A DAY during the last week or so. Now choose an hour and a minute during that day and inquire what you, Seema and Tinku were each doing at that precise moment. Discounting time differences, chances are good that you would all three have been doing more or less the same sort of thing: sitting in a schoolroom, doing homework, playing. The range of possible activities is small enough to make the probability of such a coincidence considerable.

Now apply the same test to your fathers. Tinku's father would probably be watching his tenants till a field with two plodding bullocks and a wooden plow. Or he might be sitting cross-legged on the mud floor of the kitchen at Bajitpur using his fingers to eat a meal of rice and fish curry off a big brass platter. Or he might be ducking his head under the brown waters of the pond, taking his noontime bath.

Could your own father conceivably have been doing any one of those things?

Far more likely, your father would have been engaged in

something like the sort of thing Seema's father was doing. Either one might be eating a breakfast of toast and coffee. Both might be driving his own car or motorbike to work. They might be reading a memo in an office. New Delhi may be the capital of faraway exotic India, but life there for the well-to-do is not, after all, so very different from that in other lands.

City work in India may also seem similar to city work everywhere. There are all the familiar categories: trade and commerce, manufacturing, transport, finance, domestic service and so on. But if the work most urban people in India do sounds the same as that done elsewhere, the truth is that it isn't. The tools people use, the places they work, the means by which they get there and the amount they accomplish in a day are not at all suggested by the names of the jobs they do.

Manufacturing is a good example. To an American, the word "manufacturing" means first of all machinery. He visualizes streams of workers driving automobiles through factory gates to work. He imagines miles of conveyor belts. He sees an endless stream of goods coming off a carefully planned production-line. But this is not what manufacturing means in India at all.

Mohinder Singh is a manufacturing worker. Tall, black-bearded and turbaned, he is a Sikh. Mohinder Singh works for Diamond Electronics, a Delhi firm making ovens, hot plates, hot-water heaters and other household appliances.

Six mornings a week at eight-thirty sharp Mohinder Singh waves good-bye to his wife and year-old son and bicycles off to join the thick stream of cycles, motor and pedal, flowing along his route to work. The trip takes half an hour. Mohinder Singh scoffs at the idea of using a faster-moving bus. "Faster moving once I'd get on it!" he exclaims. "But I might have to wait an hour until one came along slowly enough for me to jump aboard!

"Besides," says he, shaking his neatly wrapped head and grinning, "I'm afraid of those buses." He draws himself up to his full almost-six-foot height, a reminder of the martial heritage of Sikhs. "You take your life in your hands when you run for one."

The final portion of his journey could not be made by bus anyway. Mohinder Singh leaves the thick river of traffic near the center of the city and turns into what seems to be merely an alleyway into the courtyard of a long building. On the other side of the tunnel is a surprise: narrow streets branch off and wind past tiny booths housing stores and workshops, one after another, disappearing behind corners around which are more and more rows of shops. This is one of Delhi's large markets, completely hidden from the outside street.

Mohinder Singh cycles for several minutes before he pulls up in front of a tiny stall. He adds his bike to a stack of half-a-dozen leaning against the wall, skips over some large sheets of metal being laid out by a boy and goes inside.

No wonder that the sheet metal is lying in the street! It could never be unrolled and cut indoors. The first room of the Diamond Electronics plant is a tiny hall, hardly larger than a bathroom in the United States. Into it are crammed three handpresses and other tools, not one of them motorized.

A second room, the same size as the first one, is taken up with two kilns. Outside that room is a path along which are heaped rolls of sheet metal, reels of wire, sacks of chemicals. Everywhere men are moving about, pushing boxes outside, bringing materials inside, oiling metal-cutting shears and, in general, showing signs of preparation for a day's work. But where is that work to be done?

The only other indoor space that seems to belong to Diamond Electronics is at the top of a bamboo ladder that stands at the rear of the front room. Mohinder Singh has by now greeted his fellow workmen downstairs and is advancing toward that ladder in search of the foreman. He squeezes between the huge wheel of a press and the flaking concrete wall, swings one leg behind the ladder, carefully placing his foot sideways in the three inches of space there, and hefts the other leg onto the first rung. Then he scales straight upward.

At the top his head emerges into a loft. As he scrambles to his feet, Mohinder Singh remembers to duck his head lest he soil his turban on the damp-looking ceiling six feet above. He is facing a straight-backed chair at the foot of a row of shelves, ceiling high and piled with stationery and ledgers. This is the office. Mohinder Singh calls a greeting to the electrical *mistri*, or workman, who is puttering in his shop behind the "office." It is a single bench crowded with the delicate mechanisms of the sophisticated equipment produced on it. Mohinder Singh spots the foreman in among the completed stock, which fills the "extra" space in the loft. The handsome ovens and water heaters look like so many glittering princes who have emerged, through some incredible magic, from a miserable, crowded peasant's hovel. The foreman is counting stock. He returns Mohinder Singh's *namaste*, or greeting, and shouts a brief order to him for the morning's work.

Mohinder Singh's job is one of the most important at Diamond Electronics. He is the master mechanic, the man who cuts the sheets to size, forms them into oven-boxes or hot-water cylinders on the presses, welds them, enamels them and finishes them. He has never been formally trained, cannot read or write, has never worked elsewhere. Within the tiny premises of Diamond Electronics Mohinder Singh has learned his trade.

He came to the workshop at the age of fifteen, hired to be a helper to the half-a-dozen men who formed the total staff. He unrolled sheets of metal in the road, swept the floor and ran to fetch the endless cups of tea that the dehydrating heat of India makes so necessary for working men. By watching and helping, he became expert in every nonelectrical phase of the operation.

Today Mohinder Singh and the electrical *mistri* upstairs are the core of Diamond Electronics' twenty-four-man staff. They turn out about ten items a week, ovens one week, heaters the next, hot plates the third, depending on orders and the available storage-space. Excess stock is avoided like the plague; it would choke the little firm out of existence.

"I came from my village in Punjab as a boy, because my father thought I'd have a better chance of finding work here," says Mohinder Singh. "He was right. I could never have earned as much or lived as well there. I'm pleased with this workshop and wouldn't consider changing jobs. I'll earn more and more as the company grows, for it *is* growing and will soon shift to a large new plant outside the city.

"We've grumbled sometimes over our wages, although they're pretty high as wages go. We even listened once to a union organizer. But good jobs are too scarce for us to take the risk of joining a union." Tea breaks, working conditions and lunch hours are never issues of conflict. Tea is drunk nonstop; working conditions are accepted stoically; lunch is a companionable hour spent squatting on the floor in a corner and eating *roti* brought from home.

Daily, six days a week, between nine and five, Mohinder Singh and his fellow workers perform the uncanny miracle of producing silk purses out of sows' ears. The staff of Diamond Electronics is not alone in accomplishing this kind of magic. Small-scale industries of its kind account for a major proportion of India's manufacturing production. Without these mini-workshops Indians would have almost no pencil sharpeners. Children would never know the pleasure of seeing a windup toy bear beat a tiny drum. Hospitals would have to import their thermometers from across the seas. Few Indian house-wives know the convenience of an electric iron, but of those who do, only half as many would if it were not for small-scale industries like Diamond Electronics. More than half the staplers, ball bearings, fountain pens and pressure cookers made in India are also painstakingly fashioned by men who work with a minimum of machines, doing virtually everything by hand. The variety of goods produced in this manner is staggering. As many people are employed in these miniature industries as are on the payrolls of all of America's mammoth manufacturing plants.

Important as small-scale industries are to India, however, they are not the only type of manufacturing concerns in the country. At the other extreme are roaring steel mills, sprawling machine-tool plants, oil refineries and chemical industries, huge textile mills and other factories with the most up-to-date standards. There are not many of them, but where they do exist, they are often equipped as well as the finest plants in the world.

Technical skill is clearly not lacking in India. Manufacturing has a long history in this ancient land. In prehistoric times the area was the world's greatest producer of cotton textiles. Steel has been produced in primitive furnaces for many centuries. A few modern power-looms, jute mills, coal mines and sugar refineries were started in India more than a hundred years ago. Yet much of India today is still stuck in the age of the wooden handloom and the aboriginal blast-furnace. What has kept her from lunging forward into the age of power and steel?

Two hundred years ago, when the British conquest of India was taking place, England was a poor, tiny island. Her rocky soil sprouted little cotton, sheltered little iron ore. Indeed, most of the things needed for manufacturing were scarce in England. That very poverty of natural wealth prodded the British to develop industries that would fully utilize their precious resources. But once modern industry got rolling, it demanded more and more of the materials Britain lacked. Adventurers sailed the seas in search of stuff for the mills. In India they found what they sought . . . and much more. To the people of an island so poorly provided by nature, India seemed a bottomless cornucopia. (Trade between Europe and India had, of course, been going on for centuries. It was, remember, the search for a shorter route to India that drove Columbus to the shores of America.)

India had so much natural potential, yet no one had ever felt a need to utilize it fully. Her people lived in isolated villages. They ate what they grew, wore what they spun from cotton picked in their own fields. Village metalworkers fashioned the brass platters on which they ate, and village carpenters built the wooden looms on which they wove. Most Indians didn't know a world existed beyond their village, and the few who did know didn't care.

The coming of England fell like a heavy heel on the village-folk of India. The new British rulers taxed the farmers heavily. To raise cash for the government, the farmers sold cotton, which had always before found its way to their own backs. The British bought that cotton, shipped it to their mills in England and made cloth for Englishmen to buy. But the common people of England were poor and few in number. The machines once started could not be stopped; out poured the cloth, far more than Britishers could buy. So the canny manufacturers shipped their products back to India, where they were sold to the very farmers who had grown the cotton of which they were made. Those farmers now had no cotton for home spinning. What they wore, they had to buy. Twice over, thus, they were poorer than before: they paid the new land-tax, and they bought the clothes that had once come from their own soil and labor.

As India grew poorer, the English manufacturers and traders grew correspondingly richer. Business was good, and the English became intent on keeping it so. Educated Indians began to realize that they, too, could build power looms. They could buy the farmers' raw cotton and produce much-cheaper cloth. For their price would not include the high cost of shipping to England and back again. But by then the English were firmly in control of the Indian government. Keenly aware of the danger that Indian industrialization posed to their business, they refused to license home factories. Modern India was stillborn.

Now and then, though, an exception was made. A major one was the case of Jamsetji Tata. Tata was a Parsi banker and merchant from Bombay. He knew that no country could be free in the coming age unless it was able to produce at home the goods its people required. Tata spent his lifetime hammering away at the British bureaucracy, demanding for his people the right to produce steel. Shortly before he died, he won his case: permission was granted for Tata to build India's first modern steel mill.

His sons fulfilled their father's dreams. The beginning of the twentieth century saw the beginnings of the Tata industrial empire. Others sought, and occasionally obtained, permission to produce fast-selling, high-profit goods, like clothing or baby food or soap. But the Tatas knew that without a sound foundation such industries were castles built on sand. The sons of the Bombay banker produced steel and electricity, chemicals and machines for making machines, locomotives and mine diggers: all the things needed to make things for people to use. Only when the whole range of basic products was rolling forth from Tata factories did the directors consent to make consumer goods. Today Tata is everywhere in the shops and homes of India. From tea to soap, from fabrics to lipstick, from shaving cream to transistors, hardly an item of modern use is missing from the list of Tata-made merchandise.

But however huge Tata may be, India is far, far bigger. However much Tata produces, India needs far, far more. Even with simple arithmetic, the sum of India's dilemma can be calculated. Add to the total of Tata's production the total produced by all other industries, large and small, private and government-owned. The result falls as far short of meeting India's needs as a rocket ship propelled by a popgun would fall short of reaching the moon.

Just how far short is that? The motorcycle is one example. If a well-paid engineer decides to buy a motorcycle, he cannot simply walk into a showroom and drive away on his new bike. He must pay a deposit, put his name on a list and wait anywhere from one to five years for the manufacturers to catch up with the demand. A motorcycle dealer in Bangalore recently announced that new lists would be opened for the registration of would-be owners. So many people came to sign up that the police were called to keep order. Even so, a stampede began, and several people were killed in the crush. We've already seen how small is the demand for motorcycles relative to India's immensity, how few people in all the millions of India can afford them. Yet even so tiny a need cannot be met by India's infant factories.

Still, lack of goods is not the major hardship caused by India's industrial poverty. If a man goes to a shop to buy toothpaste, the shelves will probably be full of tubes. But only a tiny number of cityfolk and rich village-landlords buy toothpaste. Most people can't afford to; they must be satisfied with a bit of salt and a twig from a tree.

For the majority of India's people, the main effect of the paucity of industries is not that they have no things, but that they have no money with which to buy things. Poverty of industry means poverty of people. When India says that her production of steel was only 4.7 million tons in 1969, she is telling the world that millions of her daughters have nothing to wear while they wash their only sari in the nearest river; that her sons are jarred atop bullock carts with wooden wheels because they cannot afford steel rims and rubber tires, and they cannot even dream of driving tractors instead; that her little children climb *neem* trees to break off twigs because the sap is reputed to be good for the teeth and it costs 100 per cent less than toothpaste and brushes.

How can a person develop into a full, healthy human being when he remains immersed in inhuman problems? It may not be true that the people of industrialized lands are automatically happier, more complete individuals. But industrialization at least produces the possibility.

Like a clumsy puppy, an underdeveloped country trips over its own feet. India could produce half again as much steel in a year as she does, but she doesn't, in part because too few people can afford to buy the things that steel will ultimately make. Why should manufacturers produce if people can't buy? How will people buy if manufacturers don't give them jobs through which they can earn the money to buy?

Yet even making jobs is only half the battle won. Those who now work in the factories of India cannot, as a rule, afford the things they produce. So low are wages that a bicycle is as momentous a purchase for a factory worker as a motorcycle is for an office worker. A box of cornflakes, a stainless-steel pot, a stuffed teddy-bear, a second pair of shoes to wear on special occasions, a storybook for a boy who likes to read, a small bottle of perfume—the thousand little luxuries that more-affluent people call necessities—are definitely and forever beyond the depth of the worker's pocketbook.

Labor unions are active among manufacturing employees in India. They are not shy in demanding higher wages, better fringe-benefits. Neither are they slow to strike. Often, workers man a totally effective picket-line for many days, even for months. Yet in the end they usually return to work with little to show for their ordeal. Manufacturing is too unimportant a part of India's economy for bosses to be generous paymasters. Rather than share their takings with employees, they prefer to close their factory gates and invest their money in land or black-market trading. Profits are higher, troubles fewer.

Who, then, are the people who can afford the products of India's factories? Who are Seema's neighbors? They are industrialists, managers, executives, high government-officials, shopkeepers, engineers, scientists: India's elite upper-class.

The executive in the air-conditioned office earns upward of a thousand rupees a month. The worker in the plant is lucky to take home two hundred. Two hundred rupees a month pays the rent in a dark hovel filled with smoke at cooking time. It buys fever and dysentery bred of foul water, flies, mosquitoes and the closeness of a dozen souls sleeping in one tiny room. Fifteen hundred rupees, on the other hand, makes possible the possession of a house like the Gulatis', fuel and containers enough to boil drinking water, window screens to keep out vermin, motorcycles to whisk one to work. Fifteen hundred rupees a month in India, about two hundred dollars, means wealth.

If the men who manage India's scanty industry are wealthy, so also are many of the men who sell the produce of that industry. In the largest cities—Delhi, Calcutta, Bombay and Madras—most shops look very much like those in the tiniest hamlet of rural India. But appearances are deceptive. The owner of even a small alcove in a crowded bazaar can do business enough to buy his daughter a life like Seema's.

In Delhi, Chandni Chowk is the center of the shopping world. Chandni Chowk is a street, the hub of a bazaar that might have been constructed for a Hollywood film set in the "steaming, intriguing, babbling casbahs of the East." Actually, Chandni Chowk is far more workaday than appearances suggest. Skinny buildings, two or three stories high, stand wall to wall along its narrow extent. The ground floor of each is a shop, tiny in width but deep. No showcases are needed here; the fronts of the stores are open to the street, like fair booths. Any time a Delhiite needs something and doesn't know where else to find it, he goes to Chandni Chowk. Shops sell electric toasters, handcrafted brass lamps, toilets, stuffed elephants gaily decorated with tiny mirrors, plastic pants for infants, saris and fabrics, television sets: everything, in fact, except groceries.

Chandni Chowk as a street is entirely ordinary. But every day, between eleven in the morning and eight in the evening, a river of trade chokes its narrow confines and changes the street from the mundane to the fantastic. On the slow current float bullock carts loaded with bedposts, horse-drawn wagons loaded with colorfully clothed village-shoppers on a spree, beeping taxis, exhaust-belching buses, here and there a camel cart. Motorcycles, bikes and scooter rickshaws buzz back and forth through the stream like dragonflies over the surface of a river.

The variety of vehicles on Chandni Chowk would be less impressive if they all moved in only one or two directions. But they don't. A bullock pulls his cart lazily straight down the center of the street. Cars pass him right and left, whizzing happily into the lane of traffic going the other way. Face-to-face with opposition, these drivers dodge. A screeching, honking tangle ensues, and the current is halted against the barrage of crisscross traffic. Meanwhile, a three-wheeled miniature delivery-truck buzzes sharply from the center of the road toward the curb, weaving its way through stalled buses and cars as if they were so much flotsam in the path of a mosquito. Finally, the driver finds his way blocked entirely. He shrugs philosophically, flips off his ignition with his truck perpendicular to the stream in the middle of the lane, and begins idly to unload his merchandise. Drivers yell, scream, honk, shout curses. "Fool! How can you unload from the middle of the road?"

The deliveryman, straight-faced, answers, "It doesn't matter. I'll manage."

Nor does the mayhem stop at the sidewalk. Pedestrians are as thick here as motor vehicles in the road. Indeed, the two intermingle, usually in the street, sometimes on the sidewalk. Crossing streets is a game of skill and daring. If the nearest approaching-vehicle is not so near nor moving so fast that it would be impossible for him to jam on his brakes and stop, the pedestrian will risk a dash. Even those who don't want to cross it must frequently resort to the street. Dancing monkeys and their encircling audience, leprous beggars displaying toe-less feet, orange vendors trying to sell full baskets to tourists who clearly have no appetite at the moment for oranges, sidewalk vendors with ready-made shirts, cheap toys and a plethora of other goods; all conspire to usurp the sidewalk from its rightful user, the pedestrian.

Chandni Chowk's middle name is Chaos. To look at the calm faces of the shopkeepers in their stalls, though, you would never suspect it. Cool white *dhotis*, the draped pants of traditional Indians, adorn the placid bodies of the merchants as they sit cross-legged on the platforms that occupy half the length of their shops. Behind them rise the mighty mountains of their merchandise. Beside them perch trusty assistants ready at their bidding to pull out any bolt or box from the highest shelf. Above them whirl the lazy electric ceiling-fans. And before them on a long bench sit the customers. If they are good customers, they are languidly sipping cold Cokes supplied by the management. They point to a bolt of fabric, or describe a desired toaster, or inquire about the types of televisions available. The boss snaps his fingers, and the nearest aide jumps up to pull the required merchandise from a towering shelf and toss it grandly to the merchant, who displays it with a flourish before the customer. The whole show smacks of the selection of silks and brocades by grand Moghul emperors. Outside, though, chaos spins its crazy muddle in a way no Moghul ever saw.

The shops of Chandni Chowk are filled with a variety of goods. A cloth store is next to a radio shop; a brassiere and ready-made sari-blouse emporium sits beside a television repair workshop. Other more traditional markets, however, are given over almost entirely to one type of merchandise. There are bazaars for books, for automobile parts, for furniture, for baskets, for doctors, for hardware and so on. Shop after tiny shop, row upon endless row, offers exactly the same stuff for sale at crazily varying prices.

Big cities today also offer another, rarer, type of shopping. It is found in modern air-conditioned emporia. Fancy merchandise is displayed in glass showcases. Try-on rooms, cash registers, self-service and a variety of goods under one roof are innovations slowly finding their way to India. Department stores are still rarities. Some privately owned ones have been started, but the government of India is the prime mover in the field. Prices rise steadily and rapidly in India. So the government has begun a chain of "Super Bazaars," huge consumer-owned cooperative department-stores, in an effort to eliminate profiteering and inflation.

Sandwiched between the wealthy patrons of air-conditioned boutiques and the poor villagers watching bolts of cheap fabric unroll at the bazaars of local market towns, there is a tiny middle-class in India. Government employment supports a large number of the not rich, not poor minority. The term "middle class" is misleading. By the standards of the lowest grade of United States civil servant, the average government-worker in India is very poor indeed. Nonetheless, his lot is far better than that of an Indian farmer or worker. The civil servant at least rates government quarters, a tiny apartment with bathroom and running water shared by dozens of families.

The offices to which these clerks journey every morning bear little similarity to government offices in the United States. The buildings, particularly in New Delhi, are often stunning: well-constructed, imaginative, contemporary. These modern facades fool the unwary into expecting modern offices within. Instead, there are huge rooms stacked high with dusty files, boxlike wooden desks and straight-backed chairs in long, irregular rows, and yellowed fans creaking overhead. The clerks, in shirt-sleeves and sandals, seem to work in slow-motion. Languidly they pull stacks of files toward them; pause for a chat or a vacant stare at—but not out—the window, which is opaque with dirt, finally scratch a notation or two in a corner and toss the files onto stacks, which seem to have been rooted to the spot for all the centuries of India's existence. Papers are everywhere; yellow and dog-eared, coated with dust, they seem about to overwhelm and swallow the clerks. The mountains of files cast weird shadows, for light-bulbs are missing here and there; either they have blown out and nobody has bothered to replace them, or they have been carried home by the clerks. Cracked teacups and water glasses stand about on the desks and the floor. Flies cover sticky crockery. Khaki-uniformed servants sit cross-legged on chairs tilted back on two legs to rest against the greasy walls. They gossip, wiggle their bare toes and await a call for a glass of water or an order to take a file from one desk to another.

Nobody would care to work very long or very arduously in such an atmosphere of indifference and squalor. Nor do low salaries, barely enough to feed two when the earner's family is more apt to number eight, do much to stimulate enthusiasm. Most clerks are therefore adept and conscientious, above all else, at avoiding work. Offices open at ten in the morning; employees begin to trickle in around ten-thirty. Good-mornings, water drinking and opening desk-drawers take another half hour. By eleven, all is ready for work to begin—after the morning tea-break, of course. Tea is hot and must be sipped slowly; that takes close to an hour. Then it's noon, lunchtime, as everyone knows. Those who do not go home eat hasty tiffins at their desks or buy snacks from roadside stalls. Then they stretch out across their tables or in the office garden for a long snooze. By two-thirty, lunch is pretty well acknowledged to have ended. Clerks settle down to transferring papers from their in-boxes to their pending files. This work continues until three-thirty, afternoon teatime. By the time tea is over, it is nearing four-thirty, which is nearly five and closing time. Files are stashed back into drawers, and the clerks begin to stretch their legs, stiff with the long day's effort. Well before five, the office is deserted.

Like every caricature, this description is not completely accurate. There are exceptional government-clerks, the ones who are busy all day, who sincerely try to aid the people who come before them and to accomplish as much work as possible. Unfortunately, the exceptions are rare, the followers of the rule many. Bribery is generally supposed to be the only oil that will make the rusty gears of government turn, and even this lubricant all too often changes into sticky molasses in the works.

Some cityfolk thus earn their wages by not working. Another increasingly enormous group also do not work, but they get no wages. They are the unemployed. Land is too densely settled and industrial growth is too sluggish to provide work for the ever-growing number of Indians. Some turn to beggary, some live on occasional jobs. Others go to college. When they graduate, these proud engineers and holders of multiple masters degrees and doctorates cannot find work. Many westerners have scoffed at the educated-but-unemployed Indian's unwillingness to settle for manual work. That reluctance is real enough. But even if degree holders were to turn out for coolie labor, why should they be hired? Any foreman can have his pick of laborers who have always been laborers, whose backs are steeled and hands calloused to the pick and the hammer. Why should he hire instead a soft college-man, whose neck will never take the weight of a dozen bricks on his head and whose body juices would be gone after an hour or so of sweating in the hot sun?

There is nothing more abundant in India than manual laborers. Every year more and more villagers pour into the cities, ready for hard work. Villages can offer little hope of well-being to the mushrooming numbers of people dependent on them. Fallow land is unknown; the earth is tired and will not, without a boost from science, produce more. An ordinary villager is lucky if he earns two hundred dollars a year, as much as an American wage-worker may get in a week. And the Indian children who must be fed on that money usually outnumber the Americans three to one.

Even when these destitute peasants turn to manual labor in the cities, they earn little more. Work is not abundant, although a hundred people will often be employed instead of two large rock-crushing machines, fifty instead of a steamroller, thirty instead of a brick-lift. However many backs, hands and heads are needed, many more wait in the hiring lines each morning. And still more arrive on every train.

Those turned away from hiring lines often wander from door to door in search of jobs as domestic servants. Virtually every household that earns a couple of hundred rupees a month employs a servant. The government clerk who lives with his wife, six children, aged mother and widowed sister in two small kitchenless, waterless, bathroomless rooms pays wages for a woman to wash the floors and dishes daily. Imagine how tiny those wages must be! The servant usually works in half-a-dozen houses, doing her own housework in the straw-and-mud shanty where she lives early in the morning and late at night. She carries a nursing infant with her to work, setting him down on the floor while she toils, and she leaves the rest of her children at home in the care of the eldest girl. She works seven days a week. And altogether, she is fortunate to earn fifteen dollars a month.

The servant is a tired-looking, ill-dressed, ill-nourished woman. Often enough, her mistress might be her twin. Although orders aplenty may roll from the sharp tongue of the mistress, the two women recognize each other as sisters in toil. The reply can be as biting as the order. The women gossip together in the kitchen. They share each other's woes, flash anger at each other when dispirited, delight in each other's infants, and exchange potions and advice when their children are ailing. A stranger in the kitchen would often be hard put to know which was mistress, which servant.

13

Hitch a Bullock to a Plow

EVERYTHING in this world changes, said a great man, except the fact of change itself. Yet change is slow in India. And if it is slow in the industries and shops and kitchens of the city, it is even slower in the work of the village.

For as many centuries as humankind can imagine, India's farmers have tilled their fields with the same types of bullocks and plows. They have sown the same strains of paddy and reaped the same varieties of rice. They have drawn water using simple lifts and wheels constructed in exactly the same ways, powered by exactly the same breeds of cattle and camels.

The only things more ancient than the work methods of India's farmers are their rulers. Now, exactly as it was six thousand years ago, the fate of every villager is in the lap of the sun and the clouds, of the wind and the rain. Democracy may be the law of India, but the weather is a monstrous dictator overriding the writ of man and tyrannizing the villages where four out of five Indians live.

The hot weather begins in March. Every day the sun shines

in a cloudless sky, baking the earth into a cracked, dusty no-man's-land. The dirt roads of the villages, pounded by the wooden wheels of the bullock carts, turn to sand many inches deep. Dust is everywhere. People walking outside cover their nose and mouth with the ends of their saris or *dhotis*. All during April and May the heat becomes worse and worse. People rise early; without electricity to run fans, it is impossible to sleep after the sun has risen. They bathe often and sleep the long afernoons away, for by then the heat is so heavy that it is impossible to stay awake without fans. Wells go dry, and what little water remains is polluted with the germs that cause dysentery. Without deep wells and electric pumps irrigation is impossible, and so work in the fields dwindles to a halt. Heat, inactivity and constant illness wring the vitality out of people. By the end of May they can manage to do little more than search the skies languidly for signs of the coming monsoon.

Its coming is anticipated by the weatherman and the priest, each calculating by his own methods the exact date it may be expected. The first week of June sees it begin in the east, a month later in the west. The villagers solemnly tick off the days on their fingers and stare skyward. What they await is not merely the coming of rain, but the start of new life.

When the first dark clouds roll over the horizon, people point them out to one another. "It will rain," they say with cautious joy. "It will be cool." Long experience with the whimsy of the monsoon, however, makes them cautious. Those clouds might disappear as silently, as mysteriously, as they came. Or a big wind might blow them past the village, and they might unload their treasure a few miles away, over another village, with only a teasing drop or two here. Anxiety is therefore mixed with joy as the people watch the clouds grow.

Soon the sky is solid cloud. The wind rises, doors slam. Women rush to bring in laundry and babies before they blow away. Drops of water, large and hard, fall. Still, people pray silently that there will be a deluge and not a disappointment. Finally the heavenly sluices open, and rain gushes down in waves.

The heat breaks like a brittle bowl. People smile and nod to each other. "It's good rain we're having," they announce, as if it were news. "Yes, it will be good for the fields . . . if it keeps up." The farmers go back to work energetically. As small, low-lying plots fill with water, rice seeds are planted. The levels are watched minutely; every rise is nodded over and approved. Every weed is plucked, every young shoot guarded and tended by hand. Soon the paddy seedlings stand an inch or two above water.

Now clay barriers are broken, and water is guided into the larger fields. The idleness of the hot season is forgotten. Every hand is turned to pulling the seedlings, carefully so that the roots are not torn, from the seedbeds and transplanting them, equally carefully, into the large flooded-fields. Wives and children, and hired laborers, too, if the farmer can afford wages, stand ankle-deep in the water, bending stiff-kneed to plunge the delicate plants into the clayey soil. Faced with the task of carefully handling millions of seedlings, not once but twice, plucking them from the first beds and planting them in the second, most humans would shrug their shoulders and give up without beginning. Yet the farm families of India do it every year, in some places where two crops grow, twice a year, and have done so for as many generations as history records.

Leisure comes with the end of planting, but not pleasure. This is a time of worry. The monsoon might still turn contrary. The growing paddy might be inundated by too much rain or be starved by too little. On the fidelity of the monsoon, which in the past has often shown its fickleness, rests the hope of the peasants. A lost crop means a year of debt and hunger. A good crop means a year of relative peace and well-being.

If the monsoon behaves itself, the daily storms finally taper off around the beginning of September. Damp clothes get almost dry in the few hours of sun between showers. In the rays of the sun, a few months before so thoroughly detested and now so welcome, moldy spices and flour are spread to dry. The hours of sunshine grow gradually longer, the storms less severe and less frequent. One day there is no rain at all; the monsoon is over.

A quiet time of promise follows. Fall is the season of flowers. Every tree and bush competes with every other to offer the rain-refreshed earth a dazzling display of color. Every breeze of the October nights is heavy with the scent of jasmine. By December the colors of the flowers have deepened and the cool of the evenings has turned chill. People huddle under thick quilts, no longer interested in sniffing the exotic perfumes outside.

The harvest begins in late December or early January. Once again all hands are busy. The golden plants are first felled so that they may rest their grain-heavy heads for a day or two. Then the farmers and their womenfolk attack them with short-handled sickles. Every infant plant was handled by stooped men and women at transplanting time. Now the same calloused hands grasp the mature paddy, and the same backs bend as sickles are applied to stems. The dry plants are collected and tied into neat bundles. As each field is cleared, the bundles are loaded onto bullock carts and carried home. There, the courtyards ring to the smack of paddy against stone, as children beat the plants against tilted stones so that the rice-full husks roll off. The paddy is then collected, spread to dry in the sun and measured.

Now intervenes a figure whose long shadow has fallen on the whole operation: the landlord comes forward to claim his share. About two-thirds of India's tilled land is owned by people who allow others to work on their property, for a price. That price ranges from 50 to 80 per cent of the crop. Tenancy is most common in the north; many tenants, though, also own a minute amount of land themselves. In the south farmers are more apt to be freeholders, although their holdings are probably no more than an acre or two. Here, also, the systems overlap, and a man who is principally an independent farmer may also till a plot or two for a landlord.

Whatever is left after the landlord has his share is carted away to the rice mill. Even now the farmer does not relax. A freak shower or wind while his grain is on the bullock cart, or lying in the open courtyard at the mill, or on its way back home again, or waiting in the farmer's own courtyard to be apportioned, may rob him of any benefit from his year's hard toil.

At last the grain is stashed away. Part goes into clay bins, with the hope that it will suffice to feed the family until the next harvest. The rest is poured into jute bags and weighed before being loaded back on the indispensable bullock-cart and taken to market to be sold. Only when the farmer is safely at home again, with the certainty that he's gotten a fair price for his grain; only once he has paid the interest on last year's debt and hidden his remaining hoard of rupees, if there is any, in a tunnel beneath the dirt floor; only then can he sigh, light his *hookah*, or water pipe, pull his bare feet comfortably up on his *khat* and truly relax.

That is the picture of a contented farmer in February—when the weather has been good. Pity the poor farmer when it hasn't! If those first monsoon clouds blew away drily; if they brought scorching winds but no rain; or if they delivered rain but too much, so that the rivers overflowed and the baby seedlings were drowned; then that farmer sits cross-legged on his bed in February not relaxing but calculating. How much rice is left from the last harvest? How many grains of rice lie between now and hunger? How many coins still jingle in the old ragbag underneath the floor, and how much rice will they buy in the dear times that scarcity is sure to bring? How much credit has he still with the moneylender, and how much more interest can he stand to carry in the years to come? How little can his children eat before their tummies blow up with dropsy, before their legs grow weak, their hungry throats cease to complain and their bodies give up the struggle?

Occasionally the anxious peasants spare some curses for the government which, they expect, will do a minimum to help them in the troubled days to come. New Delhi boasts that old-fashioned famines, when millions were wiped out in a few months of starvation, are gone forever. To be sure, there are still hard times, but few die of them nowadays. More than that minimum, however, the government is unable to do. So massive is the suffering, so widespread the vulnerability, that enormous resources in money and efficiency would be needed to help in any great measure.

Why are the villagers of India so vulnerable? For two reasons, most people believe: poverty, and the primitiveness of farming methods. Villagers are so poor that they have no savings, nothing to tide them over in a bad year. Worse still, they are always in debt to the local moneylender. Custom allows the moneylender to charge incredible interest-rates. It is not unusual for a debtor to pay back three or four times the sum he originally borrowed. Why do villagers borrow, then? The answer is that they have no choice. Taxes are high, and they must be paid in cash. Many necessities—bullock carts and cattle, kerosene and clothing—must also be bought with coin. Yet the crop, even when it is good, is ordinarily so small that little cash survives once the landlord has his share and the moneylender his interest on past debts. Where can a villager get the cash he needs except at the usual place: the moneylender's?

The government of independent India has tried to set up banks in the villages, which will lend money at low interest-rates. Though few have actually been established, where they have been, an unlooked-for and discouraging thing has happened: many farmers continue to go to the moneylender. The moneylender is a traditional village-authority. He knows each of his debtors, decides immediately whether or not to lend them money, and when the decision is yes, hands them ready cash. The bank is a bewildering arm of that faraway, menacing creature The Government. It demands that illiterate villagers fill in long forms, then considers their requests with all the slowness of governments everywhere. Even when a peasant is willing to put up with the problems posed by the bank, what is he to do when his landlord declares: Borrow from the moneylender, my cousin, my fellow pillar of traditional village-authority, or leave my land!

Many people think that the twin problem of the villages should be approached from the other side. Every task is commonly done by man and beast, unaided by any machine more modern than the waterwheel. Why not help the tiller to improve his lot by modernizing his methods? If he uses new ways, he will grow more. If he grows more, he will earn more. If he earns more, he will need neither moneylender nor bank. Irrigation will make him less dependent on the weather; modernization will make him wealthier, happier, healthier. Great beginnings have been made by reformers who have gone to villages and given the farmers sleek pumps and shiny new tractors. A year later they have returned to find the pumps clogged with rust and the tractors standing exactly where they were parked twelve months before.

It is not simply that the farmer fears what is new. Villagers get as excited as children over a glittering new tractor or a tale of large-scale farming in the United States. But the farmer turns from these stories to regard his own land. He tills a tiny plot near the pond, another many yards away beside the ridge, a third all the way across the village. If he cultivates two acres, they are divided into five fragments. Everyone else shares the same plight. Division of land among brothers when a father dies is so common in India, and has been for so many centuries, that land tenure is fantastically complex and illogical. A bird's-eye view of the countryside reveals a mosaic of queerly shaped and odd-sized tiles.

How, the farmer ponders, can I move a tractor from field A to field B without mowing down the crops of my neighbors in between? What shall I do with the tractor when I finish a row and find that there isn't room at the end to turn around? Irrigation, too, is a fine idea. But where shall I find, and how shall I afford, all the pipe needed to carry here, there and over the hill all the water pumped by that handsome new machine?

Creation of a new technology, one designed specifically for the Indian condition, would be the obvious answer. That is happening, but slowly. Meanwhile, cooperation among the farmers, swapping and consolidation of land, would help. But stubborn tradition, not to mention peasant suspiciousness, makes this almost impossible. Each thinks: This is the land my forefathers have always tilled. If I trade it for some other, might the gods not disapprove and punish me by making my new fields barren? Besides, whispers the demon Suspicion, who can say that I won't be cheated, that the new land will be as rich and yield as well as that I now till? How about a cooperative? But I cannot read. Who can I trust to see the account books for me, so that I can be sure to receive my full due?

When closely examined, the problems of India's villages are not simply poverty and backwardness. These are there. But they cover the hard skeleton of stubborn attitudes. People are stuck in the old ways of doing things, in the old system of caste, in the old links forging the chain of class. Everybody in India talks about change. Nobody is willing to part easily with the old social system.

Yet that system does change sometimes. It has changed in Punjab. The new wealth of the peasants there began with a new wheat seed. Punjab is one of the few areas of India that is mainly wheat-growing. Recently, new varieties of seeds, some from Mexico, others developed in India, were planted there. The results were spectacular. Land that had never produced more than one bushel of wheat suddenly yielded two. Given proper fertilizers and irrigation as well, the same field blossomed with seven bushels. By combining the three major factors—seed variety, fertilizers, irrigation—some Punjabi farmers are today harvesting twice as much wheat from an acre of land as farmers in the United States.

At first villagers were reluctant to use the new seeds. Cautiously they tried tiny amounts. But when output jumped so dramatically, they could no longer resist. A 10 per cent increase might have left them doubtful and stubborn. A 100 per cent boost left them flabbergasted, but eager.

Today Punjabi farmers are not only rich by Indian standards, but they also welcome innovations in their farming techniques. Tractors are much in demand. Farmers worry that the new techniques may exhaust their land, and they are experimenting with alternation of crops to refresh the tired soil. Social custom has also begun to change. Punjabis are suddenly world-conscious. They send their sons to colleges in town, plan holidays in Japan and America, and ply their guests with imported whiskey instead of the more traditional tea and cookies. Journalists and officials have dubbed the happenings in Punjab the Green Revolution.

That revolution is far from spilling over the boundaries of Punjab, though. Most of India does not grow wheat, and the technology of rice-planting is drastically different. Moreover, the social structure of Punjab was always less stringent. Large numbers of Punjabis are Sikhs, and therefore there are fewer caste problems. Landowning rather than tenantry is the rule in Punjab, and land is not so badly fragmented into tiny plots.

The rest of India is not so open to change as was Punjab and is far from ready to join the happy ranks of the Green Revolution. Yet the whole nation is feeling some of its effect. Few farmers have escaped news of what is happening in Punjab. Villagers may have known for years that other people in other lands farm in ways more productive than are their own, but now for the first time, farmers in India are doing so. Punjab has proved the ability of technology to overcome traditional resistances. The process is neither simple nor easy. Yet how long can rice remain untouched by our century's scientific magic-wand? Already, reports have begun that a new rice-seed is being planted here and there, and that the results are encouraging.

Meanwhile, however, the farmer remains dependent on the weather, as does everyone else in the village. The landlord's income depends directly on how much grain is harvested. He visits his fields frequently, eyes the growing plants, feels the heaviness of the stalks and endlessly estimates the coming yield. An ill wind before the harvest may not mean starvation for him, but it certainly blows no good. Anything un-due in the weather sets him to figuring which of his sons must be withdrawn from school for lack of money to pay fees; whether he can still afford to pay so high a dowry for his daughter's marriage; whether his wife can have the operation she needs.

The doctor watches the weather because, in part, the land-lord is apt to decide to keep his son in school, to pay his daugh-ter's dowry—and to eliminate his wife's surgery. The doctor's services, or at least his fees, are among the first items dispensed with when times are bad in the village. Yet the doctor is never needed more than during hard times. Hunger means illness. Unruly weather sees the doctor dashing about treating beriberi, rickets and all the other diseases that come from malnutrition. Even long after food is again available, the physician is still busy with cases of tuberculosis, pneumonia, stubborn fevers, against all of which his undernourished patients can muster no resistance.

Rural doctors are busy people even when times are good. Not only is there more work to be done in the villages than in the cities, but there are also far fewer doctors to do it. Few fully trained physicians care to brave the hardships of rural life as long as better-paid jobs can be had in cities.

At least partly for this reason, village doctors are not always fully trained M.D.s. Many are homeopathic and *Ayurvedic* doc-tors. Homeopathy is a system of medicine that began in the United States but is hardly known there now. It is very popu-lar in India. Homeopathic doctors receive only two years of training. They dispense drugs in very small doses to treat most minor ailments, from colds to infant-teething. Some homeo-pathic doctors refer anything more major to a fully trained colleague. But others firmly believe that all illnesses, from hives to cancer, can be cured by the tiny doses of drugs they give. Since those drugs are both harmless and cheap, many patients are more inclined to agree with them than to risk the medical doctors' high doses and high fees.

Villagers are even more strongly drawn toward *Ayurvedic*, or folk, doctors. These men prepare local herbs in ancient ways and prescribe them. For some diseases, especially those peculiar to India, *Ayurvedic* cures are often highly effective. Analysis frequently shows that the local herb contains the same chemical that the M.D. would administer in a form manufactured by a modern drug-factory. Like the homeopathic physician, however, the *Ayurvedic* doctor should, but all too often doesn't, know his limitations. Meekly superstitious villagers, frightened of the hospital in town several miles away, terrified of X-ray machines, injections and surgery, prefer to believe that a potion prepared by a local man—whose ways are as old as the long-familiar wooden plow—will knit their broken bones and heal their ruptured appendixes.

For the same reasons villagers ill with serious disorders sometimes turn to another natural village-authority: the Hindu priest. Many believe that prayer, charms and rigidly controlled diet will cure the paralysis of polio or the blindness of cataracts. They reason: Even if the local remedies do not work, at least I will be spared the torture of braving the unknown in the faraway white temple with the red cross. If I die, at least I shall die where my friends can mourn for me.

The priest is only incidentally a curer of diseases. He maintains the village temple, officiates at weddings and important festivals, keeps the important religious almanacs. It is his task to know the rituals, in case any have escaped the knowledge of the old women who really carry on the local worship. It is also the duty of the priest to beg the means of his and the temple's upkeep from the villagers, thereby giving them a chance to acquire religious merit through giving.

In actual fact, all his other duties pale beside the remaining one: being an expert in the art of astrology. Indians, even many highly educated modern people in the most advanced of the cities, believe sincerely in the power of the stars. No important decision is made, no major step taken, no wedding date set, without first consulting the *pandit*, the learned man, to know what the stars say about it. The *pandit* calculates on which date, hour and minute a bride and groom should be married in order to give them the maximum chance of well-being in life. He tells a businessman not to sign a contract at ten in the morning on Thursday, but to wait until two in the afternoon on Saturday, lest the business fail. He figures out from the roll number of a high school boy about to take his final examinations whether or not he will pass; if the stars say he will not, the parents withdraw the candidate, let him sit at home for a year and take their chances on his getting a more auspicious roll number the next year. A farmer shrewdly reads in the sky the proper time to begin his planting, and then waits two weeks longer if the *pandit's* mysterious calculations tell him to do so. Almost every decision of life is submitted to the advice of the astrologer.

Conducting daily or weekly worship is the main task of the priest in most religions. But Hinduism is a highly individualized creed; both the priest and the members of his congregation perform the same rituals alone at home. Community worship at a temple is reserved for certain special festivals. Not leadership of rites, therefore, but astrology makes the priest an important man in the everyday life of a village.

The schoolteacher is also an important man for unexpected reasons. School, we know, occupies little of his time and concern. He attends his classroom an hour or two a day. Only in the evenings does his major function commence. Then he receives villagers, reading for them government tax notices, writing their letters to in-laws in other villages, reading three-day-old newspapers aloud. The weather affects the teacher in both his capacities. When people are most needed for work at transplanting and harvest times, his students vanish into the fields, and he declares a school holiday. When the crop is good, the peasants bring him tax notices to read in the evenings; when it is bad, he reads the labels on vials of medicine.

The schoolteacher often also plays a political role in the village. He may be an organizer for a party. Very likely, he is active at meetings of the elected village-council, the *panchayat*. Members squat solemnly on the village green while they listen to the chairman, usually a landlord, conduct business; the schoolteacher often voices the villagers' concerns, interprets for them government orders, mediates between clashes of peasants' and landlords' interests.

The only other nonfarmers in most villages are government officials: the man who is supposed to be helping farmers improve their methods, the postmaster, the insurance agent, the family-planning nurse. Most of these people spend time in the village but do not live there. They stay in a nearby town, in reality an overgrown village with a post office, a hospital and a government office clustered on the only street. These centers serve the Indian countryside as administrative headquarters. Dwellers in subdivisional and district towns are not felt to be true participants in village life, however often they may visit.

Yet these people *are* usually villagers. Few city people will accept a rural posting. Most of the country officials are consequently the sons and brothers of landlords, men who have some education and who continue to live as part of their joint families, or near them, while holding government posts. Their duties and their loyalties are thus not always identical. The government may order its officers to enforce a law limiting the amount of land a person may own and transferring whatever extra a landlord has to his tenants. But if the too-rich landlord is the officer's older brother or cousin, and if the landlord declares that there is no extra land at all (as he usually does), then the officer accepts his word without blinking. Similarly, the man whose job it is to distribute fertilizer to tillers is apt to distribute it first to his father and his uncles and then to inform the peasants that he has "no stocks." The dispenser of emergency rations during a famine sees to it that his own people eat, and eat well, first, before he releases anything left over to the villagefolk. Even if the local landlords are not his kin, they are sure to be his friends.

Whoever the villager may be, it is clear, even if he is an employee of a far-distant government, he is still tied to the land. His mind is formed by his family and his caste; his life is regulated by the great tyrant: weather. Tiller and landlord, schoolteacher and priest; each lives as his ancestors lived. The tax collector may arrive on a bicycle rather than in a man-carried palanquin or carriage. But the majority of the village-folk still plod their way to market along narrow, dusty paths in a bullock cart.

Yet the Green Revolution is on its way; technology and change are coming. The bullocks of most villagers have yet to leave the ancient paths, have not yet been exchanged for a machine. But the rural folk know that change is coming nearer and nearer to their villages. Sooner or later they, too, must move into the twentieth century.

A camel cart in a street in New Delhi

A section of Chiltaranjan Locomotive Works, Bahar

Apprentices in Tata Iron and Steel Company's training center

Loading coal manually onto a ship in Calcutta port

Changing from a railway terminus into a steamer, West Bengal

Potter's shop, Jaipur, Rajasthan

A Rajasthani cloth-retailer in his shop

Craftsman painting toys, West Bengal

Stone-carver making idols, Onissa

Folk dancers, Punjab

Peasant rally in a Punjab village

Election day, Bombay. Campaigning volunteers on truck distributing cold drinks to crowds

Harvested paddy field, West Bengal

An open-air bath in working-class tenement in the industrial suburbs of Calcutta

Students lined up to see a movie, Calcutta

View of Bombay from Malabar hill

Fishermen on the beach in Puri, Onissa, on the Bay of Bengal

14

The Skill of Ages:
Arts and Crafts

"DIVERSITY WITHIN UNITY" is one of the clichés used to describe India. It suggests nothing less than the truth. India is like an optical puzzle: viewed one way, it seems all difference, dissimilarity, paradox. But viewed another, it is all harmony: profound oneness.

From the angle of culture, it is the unity of the land that presents itself. Ways of dressing, ways of making things, ways of cooking, of singing, dancing, sculpting, painting, are all distinctively Indian. Indian designs and patterns, color schemes and shapes, when found anywhere in the world, are immediately identifiable as Indian.

Yet nowhere is the diversity of the land more real than in its crafts and cultures.

Foremost and most famous among the crafts of India is the manufacture of textiles. India's fabrics have been loved for as long as history has been recorded. Job's wisdom, says the Old Testament, is more lasting than Indian dyes. Nero's court called Indian muslins *nebula venti* ("woven winds"). Another

Roman emperor complained that fine ladies of his court were depleting his gold reserves by importing these muslins in such huge quantities. Even when the Roman Empire was in its infancy, the art of dyeing was ancient in India. Researchers digging out the prehistoric cities of the Indus Valley have found traces of cloth dyed in exactly the same way it is done today.

No less incredible than the age of dyeing methods is the variety. Special designs and intricate patterns are achieved by hundreds of different highly skilled techniques. Best known among them today are tie-dyeing and *batik*.

A common idea of tie-dyeing is that bunches of material are gathered together, tied off and then dipped in dyes. That is an oversimplification. There are at least two ways of tie-dyeing. In *patola*, large-pattern tie-dyeing, it is the unwoven fibers that are bunched and dipped. Warp and weft threads are separately stretched on frames, sketched with the pattern, usually a geometric one, tied and dyed. Then the two are woven so that like colors fall together. The matching can never be exact, and so the edges of the pattern become blurred and subtle, giving *patola* weaves their distinctive look.

Bandhani is another form of tie-dyeing practiced all over India, but particularly in Rajasthan. *Bandhani* dyers do actually tie the finished fabric, usually a very thin cotton. But rather than bunching the fabric, they pinch tiny dots together, twisting thin threads around the raised material. The finished tie-dyed cloth is covered with rows and rows of minute raised dots, which form intricate patterns. So full is the cloth of tied areas that the whole scarf or sari has a puckered, springy texture to it.

The *batik* method uses a different principle to protect some parts of a cloth while dyeing others. The areas not to be dyed are painted with molten wax. Then the fabric is dipped in vats of cold dye. As the material is handled, the wax cracks and ribbons of color appear in the waxed spaces. Then the piece is washed in hot water, melting the wax to expose the undyed areas. Now the cloth is again painted with wax, leaving new areas exposed. Again it is dipped in dye, a different color this time. The process is repeated over and over again, until the whole piece is dyed. One color reacts on the others used before, so the exact result can never be calculated in advance. Yet the crinkly, smudged patterns and figures of *batik* printing are rarely anything but exquisite.

Batik is an old method of printing saris and scarves. It is also used to produce paintings. Lately *batik* has become a favored medium for modern artists who combine contemporary styling with traditional symbols.

Batik is a long and tedious process. The beginner is amazed at the patience it demands. Yet the labor needed for *batik* is child's play compared with the effort that goes into the embroidery work of Kashmir.

Kashmir, a state in the far northwestern corner of India, lies entirely in the Himalaya Mountains. At its heart is the glorious Kashmir Valley, a long strip of flatland high in the hills, filled with rivers and lakes and surrounded by mighty peaks. Kashmir boasts its own history, its own language, its own distinctive cultural style. During the summer months the state is alive with trade and farming, and especially with the vacationing visitors who arrive in swarms from the torrid plains. But for the other half of the year Kashmir is snowbound and deserted. Kashmiris, among the poorest people and most skillful craftsmen of India, occupy themselves with weaving and embroidery work during those long winter months.

A single woolen scarf may be embroidered with hundreds of thousands of stitches, a dozen hues making up a delicate pattern of leaves and flowers. Kashmiri wool is the softest in the world. Unadorned, its weight is feather-like. But a shawl may be so heavily embroidered that the tiny threads of the design together weigh two or three pounds. So skillful are Kashmiri embroiderers that they can create reversible shawls, with the pattern identical on both sides but in different colors. Sometimes they split the thread of the wool as they work, so that the finished article is heavily embroidered on one side but bare on the other.

Elegant as India's cottons and woolens may be, silk is the fabric for which the land is most noted. "The silks of India" is a phrase evocative of all the richness and glamour of the East. Every part of India produces silk, and each has its own style and quality. From Murshidabad, in Bengal, come light-weight gaily printed materials; from Benares, more-satiny fabrics dyed in deep tones and richly embroidered with gold or silver threads; from Bangalore, thick, luxuriously patterned and colored silks; from the south, rough, subtle-hued, elegant tussore silk.

The very profusion of the stuff indicates how much a part of life it is in India. Silk is bought to be worn, not hidden away in boxes and drawers. Wealthy women wear silk saris daily during the cool winter months. Every middle-class woman has a variety of silks from which to choose when she sheds her ordinary cotton sari in order to go visiting. No Durga Puja is complete in Bengal without a new Murshidabad sari for each woman of households that can afford them. Even some peasant women have silk marriage saris to treasure, bringing them out for every *puja* and wedding. A girl who is married in cotton is a poor girl indeed, hardly consoled by the fact that most of the brides of India are too poor to afford silk.

Silk can be machine-made. But most often it is handloomed. The pattern can be woven into the fabric on the loom or stamped on with blocks later or printed by *batik*. Silver or gold threads can be woven with the silk fiber. Solid-colored silks are often embroidered, with gold threads in Benares, with cotton threads in Kashmir. Kashmiris used to make tablecloths and bedspreads in this way. Huge medallions, rich blends of deep purples, blues, reds, oranges and browns, filled the centers of these masterpieces. One of these medallions, issuing from a mean peasant-hut in the Kashmiri hills, could easily have been framed and hung in the world's noblest palace. Today the work is hardly done, for few modern homemakers care to use anything as elegant as silk for such workaday purposes.

Where the rich Kashmiri medallions are still commonly to be found is in the center of pile carpets. India is one of the major producers of rugs. Floor coverings have traditionally played a far more important role in Indian life than in western culture. People of an earlier day valued them not as decorative luxuries but as substitutes for furniture.

Until recently, though (recently, that is, in the Indian scale of time), pile carpets were unknown in the land. The first references to Indian pile carpets are found in records from the fifteenth century, a mere five hundred years ago. They were introduced into the country from Iran. Indian weavers quickly began to make them, using Indian motifs and designs, such as the Kashmiri medallion. Kashmiri carpets today are among the finest produced anywhere in the world, containing as many as 450 knots in a square inch.

Throughout the eastern ranges of the Himalayas, mountain-folk make carpets. Although citizens of India, these hill people are often culturally closer to China, on whose border they live. The patterns of their carpets combine the styles of both great lands.

The Himalayan carpet-weavers are usually women. Kashmir is an exception. There, following the custom of the plains, men practice the craft. Most Indian handicrafts are the preserve of men in one place, of women in another. Where women produce crafts that are important to the economy of the region, the social effects are often notable. In Chanderi, for instance, the ladies work the looms, and the local people chant:

> In the kingdom of Chanderi, where weavers dwell,
> Women rule, while men fetch water from the well.

Some crafts involve a joint effort by husband and wife. Both men and women embroider in Kashmir, although the hereditary master-craftsmen are men. To produce *bandhani* tie-dye, women tie and men dye.

Cooperation between the sexes is also the rule for such crafts as pottery and basketmaking. The latter is very often done by non-Hindu tribal people. Originally hillfolk, many among the forty million tribal people have, over the centuries, moved down to the plains. There they settled in villages like Bajitpur, living side by side with the Hindu and Muslim residents. The tribal people excel as workers in reed, making elaborately patterned baskets and mats. The women split the bamboo poles, the men plait the baskets. With a dozen rings in their ears and noses jingling playfully, the women keep the pace with a mixture of song and banter. The men follow their instructions about size, shape and pattern of the pieces they weave.

Among potters, the order of importance of the sexes is reversed. The woman prepares the clay and paints the finished pots, but the man works the wheel and molds the bowls. The potter's equipment, which is little more than sticks and stones, is a masterpiece of simple ingenuity. With it he can produce wares of uncanny precision at high speed.

Although Bengal and Kerala today produce fine ceramic-work and china, glazing is not a traditional craft of India. Most clay pottery is used unglazed, fired once and sometimes decorated with colored slip or paints. Religion probably influenced the potters' lack of interest in glazing. Hindus, with their enormous emphasis on ritual purity, do not believe that clay utensils can be truly cleaned. They do not mind storing rice or flour in clay pots, but it is another matter to eat from a plate that has been used before by someone else. Small clay cups called *kulhar* are used in tea shops and by vendors of food at railway stations. But they are dispensable, tossed with a dash against the ground once used. *Kulhar* shaped exactly like modern ones have been dug up in the Indus Valley cities. Imagine how many billions of cups have been smashed in the five thousand years since then!

Rather than eating from pottery utensils, Hindus prefer to use brass ones. Brasswork is among the most highly developed of Indian crafts. The range of products stretches from everyday platters to elegantly nonfunctional vases inlaid with colored metals in elaborate designs. Certain shapes are classical, such as that of the graceful *kolsi*, or water jug. Round-bottomed so that it can be tipped without lifting, its neck thin for gripping and its mouth wide for pouring, the *kolsi* is ideally designed to be filled from the well or dipped in the pond, then swung onto a female hip or head and carried home to a tapless mud house.

It is surprising that Indians, who have managed to produce so little steel in this modern age of steel, are age-old experts in metalworking. Idols and vessels cast in Mahenjadaro fifty centuries ago are identical with those made in India today. The ancient Persians defended themselves against the invading armies of Alexander the Great with weapons hurriedly imported from India, the world's major manufacturer of quality metals at the time. Near Delhi there stands a twenty-four-foot-high iron pillar. It is fifteen hundred years old . . . and has not a spot of rust on it! Scientists have tested it in every possible way, yet cannot understand what protects it from the elements. Equally baffling is the riddle of where the pillar was cast. The earliest foundry known to have been large enough to produce such a massive piece of iron was built four hundred years after the pillar had already been erected.

Nor have Indians historically been behind in their knowledge of the techniques of steel-smelting. Many centuries ago tribal people knew how to make steel in primitive blast-furnaces, and they continue to produce the metal for their own use in the same way today.

The long tradition of metalworking explains one paradox of modern India. Motorbikes and automobiles are cared for by skilled mechanics who handle their tools as if they were extra fingers on their hands, who know how to improvise, to make parts that cannot be bought, to substitute a not-quite-right bolt for a missing one, who seem, in short, to have mastered their trade as thoroughly as the makers of bullock carts have theirs. In fact, the mechanics and the village craftsmen are of the same genre. Both are artisans, practicing skills learned not from books but through apprenticeships. Both have been born to their craft, and each expects his son to pick up his tools when the time comes. The fact that India can offer the services of skilled technical-people to the owners of motorbikes does not mean, in other words, that India has become modernized. All it means is that India has absorbed the most advanced technology into her ancient pattern of craftsmanship.

If the line between ancient craft and modern skill is blurred and wavy, no clearer is the one separating manufacturing from art. The brass *kolsi* dipped daily into the muddy waters of the pond outside Tinku's house in Bajitpur would be equally at home holding an artful arrangement of cat-o'-nine-tails in the living room of a Manhattan apartment. The clay image of Durga before which Tinku's grandmother bows her head each fall is second-cousin to the famous dancing Shiva in a Madras museum. Both sculptors were nameless craftsmen who had learned their skills not in art schools but at the dusty knees of their fathers.

No finer examples of Indian art can be found than the cave temples at Ajanta and Ellora, near the city of Aurangabad, in central India. Monks of the Buddhist sect began to build a monastery for themselves at Ajanta in the second century B.C. Lying in lushly wooded hills, the location offered serenity and isolation but little in the way of accommodation. The monks determined to dig caves out of the side of a horseshoe-shaped cliff. For nine hundred years they worked at it. Bit by bit the cliff was chipped away to form twenty-nine caves.

Spectacular as the feat of excavation alone is, it pales beside the wonders that the Buddhist monks created inside. On the walls of the caves were painted pictures so marvelous that Ajanta is today one of the world's great centers of art. In colors now faded but once vivid and sharp, the people of India live, eat, sleep, love, wash, put on lipstick, play and meditate. Massive murals depict complex scenes from Buddha's life. One tells the story of Buddha's meeting with his mother when he returned to his palace as a beggar. Another depicts the death of Buddha's sister-in-law after her husband had left her to become a monk. So vital is the drawing that the woman seems to slip from life to death just at the moment the visitor to Ajanta reaches that spot.

Other paintings illustrate the Buddhist fables. A kindly king, for example, shelters a pigeon fleeing from a hawk. The pursuer accuses the king of depriving him of his natural prey. The king, who is known widely for his sense of justice, settles the dispute by measuring out and presenting to the hawk a quantity of his own flesh equal to the weight of the pigeon.

Throughout the frescoes there are scenes of daily Indian life that might be happening today in the marketplaces or the fields near Ajanta. Hawkers cry their wares. Women select fruits. Young girls gracefully carry water jugs on their heads. People bathe themselves in rivers. A court beauty carefully paints her lips. Ajanta is as much a comment on the continuity of Indian life as it is a tribute to the genius of the artists who created the frescoes.

Most of India's many temples and monasteries are decorated not with paintings but with sculptures. Walls are often *bas reliefs* active with elephants, horses, bulls, gods and goddesses. When Ajanta was abandoned (for reasons nobody has yet discovered), the monks moved to Ellora, another mountain site not far away. In time, that monastery passed on to Hindus, who created there one of the many great sculptural wonders of India. It is the Kailasa, a replica of the mythical mountain housing one of Hinduism's major gods, Shiva. Working for over a hundred years, craftsmen cut away three million cubic feet of rock to form an enormous cave. Inside it are three temples connected by an overhead bridge, all carved from the same solid hill. For all its massiveness, the cave contains detailing as fine as one might find on a miniature, and an overall unity of design as harmonious as that of a Japanese tea house. India is often criticized, with perfect justice, as a land of disorganization. Yet imagine the organization needed over a period of an entire century to *carve*, not construct, all that complexity within a mountain. Not a single bridge or statue was added to the cave. From top to bottom it was slowly chiseled out, according to one plan.

Sculpture and painting draw heavily on mythology and literature for their subjects. So plentiful is the well of Indian literature that it might be drawn upon, *has* in fact been drawn upon, for many, many centuries without being the least depleted. From the great Hindu classics, the *Ramayana* and the *Mahabharata*, through the tales of modern writers, a reader—or, as is more common in India, a listener—can be entranced and delighted for as long as he cares to pay attention. For children, in addition to the inexhaustible epics, there are the enchanting fables of the *Panchatantra*.

Modern writers seem often to have lost the skills of their forefathers. Without the rake of time to scrape away the mediocre works and leave cleanly exposed the living blades of genius, many leaves clutter and obscure the true works of art. Modern India is blessed, though, with one genius so profound that no amount of lesser work by contemporaries could obscure his greatness. He was Rabindranath Tagore, a man whose talent recognized no fences but wandered freely through all the lanes and fields of creativity. He was above all a poet who produced thousands of poems, long and short, each of a language so polished and a conception so keen that any one alone would have won him an enviable reputation. He also wrote short stories, novels and plays. He painted. He established an experimental university. He began a form of dance-drama that combines ballet and opera. He wrote music, creating an entirely new school of singing. He composed the national anthem, which is also a fine example of Tagore's skill in capturing the gliding beauty of his mother tongue, Bengali: It begins:

> *Jana gana mana adhinayaka jaya hey*
> *Bharata bhagya vidhata.*

> Thou art the ruler of the minds of all people
> Dispenser of India's destiny.

Between the rhythm of Tagore's poems and the beat of music, the line is very thin. Indian music has enormous variety, from the religious dirges called *kirtan* to the snappy songs of the modern movie. Through it all runs, however, a common strand. The basic sound is different from any known in the West. Indian music has a plaintive air about it. It suggests sorrow and meditation. Yet it can also be gay and its rhythms so magnetic that the listener cannot help bouncing, tapping and drumming in time.

Movement is, in fact, the expected response to music in India. Audiences are not supposed to sit stock-still in stuffy concert halls. Musical evenings are casual affairs, often held in a courtyard or a garden. Whole families attend, people come and go, chat quietly and, most of all, move to the music. They drum on the floor (on which they sit), on their own arms, on the backs of their neighbors, on anything within reach.

From rhythmic motion comes dance. The variety in Indian dance is as astonishing as the variety everywhere else in Indian life. What a surprise that the controlled, stylized, meticulous foot-motions of *kathak* can belong to the same land as the dance of Assam in which some girls beat the rhythm on the ground with long crisscrossed sticks while others hop nimbly in and out of the disappearing spaces in between!

The number of different kinds of entertainment available in this land of drab poverty is amazing. Folk drama is an ancient art, still very much alive in the villages, where the arrival of a wandering troupe of actors is a titillating event. Villages of snake charmers continue to train their sons to this traditional skill. The musicians catch and defang the reptiles, then play to them the haunting flute melody that identifies their particular art. The audience is generally more charmed by the tune than are the snakes, but the latter shadow the weaving motion of the instrument as it is played. Trained monkeys compete with trained bears, puppet masters with acrobats, magicians with circuses, and fortune-tellers outdo them all.

Each entertainer is carrying on the traditional skill of his fore-fathers. In this he is like the craftsman who weaves age-old patterns into his silks or hammers brass water jugs in timeless forms. Most entertainment in India, like most handicraft, is exactly what it was five thousand years ago.

Yet we have seen that the list of crafts is not static; the skill of the motor mechanic has been added in this century. So also has traditional entertainment been embellished by a modern addition: the movies. Tinku's older cousins in Bajitpur long for the rare times they can see a movie in the nearest theater, twenty miles away. They envy the town dwellers and hungrily ask each new acquaintance, "Is there a cinema where you live?" A girl's idea of bliss is to be married into a family which lives near a movie theater. Young ladies sigh for leading men, recount in detail plots of old films, discuss endlessly the new arrivals. In their passion for the movies, they are indistinguish-able from Seema and her friends.

Most Indian films are, by American, European or Japanese standards, old-fashioned, melodramatic and horribly overacted. The threatened heroine clutches her breast, presses the back of her wrist to her forehead and exclaims, "Alas, I am lost!" Sor-rowful voices quaver. Grievous news is received by fainting. Kisses are prohibited on the screen. Lovers proclaim their feel-ings by rolling their eyes.

India's movie industry is one of the biggest in the world. Hindi movies are made in Bombay; Bengali movies in Cal-cutta. Among the Bengali films are some that are exceptional: up-to-date, dramatic, pensive, insightful. Satyajit Ray is the most famous master of the modern Bengali cinema. His *Apu Trilogy*, three films tracing the life of a poor *Brahmin* boy from a village, placed him among the world's leading directors.

When we come to the cinema, that optical puzzle, India, seems to hop out of phase. Crafts, arts, and entertainment seemed to be the great binding-agent which, by composing India's culture, defined her oneness. Actually, though, a Rajasthani sweeper probably knows nothing of Kashmiri embroidery, nor a villager in Tamilnadu anything of the *kathak* dance style in the north. What does *really* unite them is their enthusiasm for the latest movie. India laughs at simple attempts to understand her. It is, after all, not her ancient culture, but that new import from the West, the cinema, that links all her people in a common love.

15

The Building of the Road

IT IS THE people of India, more than anything else, that display her diversity. If Gopal the beggar-boy were to meet the Raja of Jubbal one day, he would find nothing to say to him beyond, "Give!" These two, both born in India, might live on different planets for all they seem to have in common. Seema and Tinku—one the offspring of the city, the other of the land—have little more about them to show that they come from the same nation.

Yet each one of the four—beggar, raja, well-to-do city girl and boy of the mud-hut village—feels that his place in India is natural, that there is nothing strange or alien about his being what he is. Each one is right. They are like travelers on the same express bus. Their lives may touch each other not at all, or only superficially. Yet they travel together. They share the same bit of road. They have started from the same place, and they are hurtling toward the same terminus. The bus is the day-to-day events of India; the road is the long and complex history of the land, which has paved the way for today and stretches far ahead into the future.

The road to the past stretches far back to the birth of human civilization. We have noted before how old the Indus Valley civilization is. Nobody knows exactly who the people of the ancient Indus Valley were. But their cities were already well developed so many thousands of years ago that the question is not very important. Their civilization almost certainly grew to maturity influenced only by Indus Valley conditions. Signs abound that the people who live today in south India, the Dravidians, are of the same stock as the Indus Valley civilization people. Popular theory has it that today's south Indians were very early migrants from the north.

It *is* known that a new strain of humanity invaded from the northwest about a thousand years after the Indus Valley cities had ceased to flourish, overcome, probably, by changes in the course of the river and the consequent creeping intrusion of the desert. The Aryans, probably through forays that gradually grew in power over long periods of time, conquered the Dravidian people. Like so many later conquerors of India, they merged with their defeated enemies to form a new civilization. Yet the two strains, living together, also conflicted with each other. The Dravidians had behind them thousands of years of advanced civilization. The Aryans, relatively much closer to barbarism, nonetheless considered themselves to be superior. The religion of the Dravidians, identical in essentials to the Hinduism of today, seems to have been adopted as the creed of the conquerors. Yet the roots of caste probably go back to the Aryans' attempt to set themselves above their subjects.

Cities had dominated the culture of the Indus Valley civilization. With the victory of the Aryans, the village came into its own. Exact information on how people lived is lacking. But indications are that the village as it is known today was forged at that time. Bullocks were used to plow. Paddy was grown.

The village community was self-sufficient, governed effectively by its own council of elders. Families were joint. In most of India, the oldest man ruled his brothers, all the women of the household and all the offspring. Many areas, however, were matriarchal, and women held the authority within the family. Even today, in some parts of the far south and the far north, mother-power is the rule.

The very early political system of India can only be vaguely guessed at. Probably there was a diffuse network of very small monarchies. The leaders were more like local chieftains than like the glittering maharajas of more recent times. A trend toward consolidation, however, soon began, and by the fourth century B.C. the age of empires had become well established.

The accomplishment was that of Chandragupta Maurya, a raja who warred against all the other kings of north India and won. He established a tight administration, centralized and demanding. In the cities the dicta of the absolute monarch touched almost every aspect of life. The sturdy villages, however, were hardly affected. Chandragupta's books did contain rulings that governed agriculture. But real rural power remained stubbornly in the hands of the village council, which was often locally elected.

Chandragupta's empire passed in time to his grandson Asoka. Asoka was a Buddhist. At first he was also a keen warrior. It was his ambition to complete his grandfather's work, to conquer every part of the subcontinent not yet subdued. He waged war efficiently, and soon only two enclaves remained outside his sway: an eastern region and the southern tip of the land. Asoka sent an expedition to mop up the isolated easterners. Soon the news arrived that one hundred thousand people had been slain, one hundred fifty thousand made captive, and the war decisively won. Great rejoicing was in order, but something suddenly happened to the king. Abruptly, in a flash of enlightenment reminiscent of Buddha himself, Asoka experienced a change of perspective. Those thousands of sufferers, those insignificant pawns in the game of conquest, suddenly grew before his eyes to the stature of men and women. No more were they servile subjects newly come under his heel. Now they were nothing less than human beings in travail.

Instead of declaring the opening of the next campaign, against the only remaining independent territory in the south, Asoka announced that war would never again be waged in his empire. India thus remained disunited and has never been one to this day. Asoka spent the rest of his life converting his followers to Buddhism, trying to attain for them "security, self-control, peace of mind and joyousness." His reign was famous everywhere for its gentleness and good works.

After Asoka came a new wave of invasions. First came the central-Asian Scythians and then another Asian people, called the Kushans. The Kushans eventually ruled much of north India. Conquerors and overlords though they were, they soon took up Indian ways. The people whom they had beaten with arms now overcame them with culture. Conqueror and conquered became indistinguishable.

Nonetheless, the rule of these outsiders crystallized a nationalist feeling. Previously, the upper classes of India had warmly enjoyed the exchange of culture and knowledge that attended their international trade and that thrived in their multi-national centers of learning, places like the great university at Taxila. Now, they began to turn away from these contacts, to withdraw into their "Indian-ness."

In the fourth century A.D. a second Chandragupta pushed out the Kushan rulers and established a new empire. It extended, however, only as far as the mountain range that separates north and south India. In the south, several important and independent kingdoms had meantime arisen. The southerners, unconquered by foreigners, were themselves colonizers. They conquered Ceylon and southern Burma and, in support of their abundant overseas trade, set up colonies throughout Asia.

In the north the empire of the Guptas flourished for a century and a half. This period is called the Golden Age of Indian culture and philosophy. Political security opened a cornucopia of progress in the sciences and arts. Mathematics, for instance, was enriched by the development of algebra. Aryabhata, an astronomer as well as a mathematician, wrote the first known book on algebra in the fifth century A.D., when he was only twenty-three years old. From India came such invaluable concepts as zero, using letters to indicate quantities, negatives, squares, cubes and their roots. Combined with the use of decimals, another Indian invention, algebra unlocked the door to all of higher mathematics and with it to all of latter-day technology. Medicine, chemistry, the science of political administration, sexology, almost every possible field was furthered by the achievements of Indian scholars during this time.

The ferment of thought and creativity in the Guptas' India did not, however, prevent a tightening of the social and economic systems. Caste and other elements of the social system became more rigid. As a result, one area of thought after another, having produced work of incomparable majesty, proceeded to dry up like a dead geyser. By the eighth century Indian science and philosophy were barren. Letters and art were barely more interesting. Foreign trade had fallen off; and the political dominion of the Guptas had broken up into petty kingdoms. Constantly at war with each other, their borders forever shifting, their armies perpetually trampling the young crops of the peasants, these kingdoms were easy prey to new waves of invaders from other lands.

The change in India can be gauged from the comments of visitors about the people of the land. When Alexander invaded India in the fourth century B.C., his historian Arrian commented on the gaiety of the people: "No nation is fonder of singing and dancing than the Indians." Fourteen centuries later, a ruler named Mahamud from Afghanistan raided his neighbor to the east. In his entourage there traveled a scholar named Alberuni. Alberuni reported that the Indians were "haughty, foolishly vain, self-contained and stolid." *

The result, as Mahamud's raids proved, was that invaders found north India an increasingly easy place to conquer. A succession of Muslims came from different places. First came more Afghans who captured Delhi in the thirteenth century. Then Timur the Turk rolled lustily through the land, leaving corpses and cinders behind him. Finally, Babar, a mixed descendent of Turkish and Mongolian Muslims, came and established the rule of the Great Moghuls, which was to continue for another two hundred years.

Much has been made by religious partisans of the ability of Muslims to conquer Hindu India. At the time, though, it must have seemed a most natural event. India had pulled in her skirts and withdrawn into a finicky isolation. Islam, on the other hand, was young. Having arisen in the deserts of the Middle East, it had boisterously expanded in Europe, where Christianity was deep in the doldrums of the Dark Ages. In all the world the brightest intellectual light shone from the Muslim university at Cordoba in Spain, as it once had from Taxila in India. While every other people seemed old and stolid, youthful Islam rampaged and conquered.

Those warlike Moghuls, though, proved themselves to be masterful administrators. For all the carnage that marked their

* Quoted by Jawaharlal Nehru, *The Discovery of India*, Asia Publishing House, 1961, pages 122 and 248.

marches through India, the empire they finally established gave to the land another two centuries of peace.

Peace, of course, is a relative term. While the people were peaceful, the emperors warred. Rarely has history recorded so bloody a series of assassinations and conspiracies in high places as stud the annals of Moghul rule in India. Great monuments were built: notable among them the Taj Mahal in Agra, memorial of a bereaved emperor to his queen, who died bearing her fourteenth child. But however much they constructed, however steadfastly they administered their subjects, they could not build a smooth path from one generation of emperors to the next. Most successions took place with a new rush of gore and brutality.

Still, India flourished under the Moghuls. No spectacular accomplishments can be chalked up to the time. Yet visitors to Moghul India were impressed by the refinement of the court, by the frictionless ease of village relations, by the throb of trade and the skills of artisans who worked under the protection of the administration.

Someone unbiased who had traveled in India and then journeyed on to Europe would have been struck by the contrast. In Europe, by the beginning of the seventeenth century the plight of France's tillers had become desperate, and the seeds of revolution were being sown right and left. England's landowners were enclosing village lands and forcing those made destitute in the process into city slums. To survive, these landless folk slaved in dark factories sixteen hours a day, then returned to homes where, according to British government medical officers, far less air was available than a human being required to remain fully alive. Wars among the nations of Europe were frequent. More and more, those conflicts were extending to the lands beyond the continent, as the race for colonies got under way.

Yet it was crude Europe and not refined India that was to win the contest for dominance in the coming age. Exactly that crudity of life in Europe was forcing society to find new ways of existing, ways that India found to be unneccessary. In 1760 the city of Dacca in East Bengal produced the finest muslins in the world. What need had the craftsmen of Dacca, well fed, respected men all, for the flying shuttle that was that very year beginning an amazing transformation of the textile industry of England?

On the other hand, the British, the French and the other industrially developing European nations had need of something that India could offer in super-abundance: cotton and other raw materials, and markets where could be sold the miraculously multiplied output of the industrial revolution. In the struggle for India, the British soon won. The Moghul emperors still sat upon their Delhi throne, but their power was gone. The British, at this time represented by the East India Company, a commercial organization of traders turned conquerors, contracted with the emperor at Delhi to be his agents. In his name they warred with resistant kingdoms elsewhere in the subcontinent.

The battle was not easy, but its outcome was certain from the first. The Indians were divided among themselves. Various rajas vied with each other for prominence. They mistakenly believed that the interests of the British were not political but only commercial. So they allowed their rivalries to impede their war prowess. The British, on the other hand, were quietly establishing administrative control of the areas they conquered. Whole states were bought by treaty agreements with helpless or greedy rajas. Still in the name of the Moghul emperor, the British were silently building their *raj* in India.

By the middle of the nineteenth century, the conquest of

the land was complete. Using an army manned by Indians, the British controlled, directly or by treaty, the whole of the country. Yet resistance was not dead. A group of daring soldiers, aided by some rajas who still refused to come to terms with the East India Company, rebelled in 1857. Throughout north India they turned against their British officers, overthrew the administration and cast terror into the hearts of the rulers. For a few days, the fate of British rule seemed to hang by a thread. But the rebellion had little active support beyond the army, and the coterie of rajas who had originated it. It was a flash of proud anger, and it died as it had come, quickly and bloodily. For every Britisher killed, the Company hanged hundreds of Indians. For long afterwards the highways of the land were shaded by gallows.

Only after the rebellion did the British government transfer control of the land from the East India Company to the king. India became a colony in name, as it had been in fact for a century before.

What kind of rulers were the British? Compared to those who had come immediately before, they would seem at least to have given the country some sort of political calm. That, at least, is what the British themselves claim. Yet that calm was dearly bought. The price was a basic distortion of the economic life of the country. Beyond question the British colonization of India, as we have seen before, affected the lives of the simple villagers adversely. It killed the local crafts and thereby pierced the skin of village self-sufficiency. At the same time, it tied cultivators more strictly to their land and their landlords than ever before. And it sank them in the mire of usury by imposing taxes that could only be paid in cash.

At the same time the British created a railway system unparalleled in Asia. To every crevice and point on the map of India ran the monster *chook-chook gharry*. Without it, how could the British export raw cotton and import finished cloth? More important still, how could so few Britishers ensure their control of so many millions if every town and village were not accessible to police and army?

In the tally of colonialism, pluses and minuses can be chalked up forever. The British claim that they dragged backward India into the modern world. Indian nationalists counter that India would have found her way there anyway . . . and much faster had Britain not forbidden the building of industry in the land. Others wonder whether India has truly entered the modern age at all. The British boast that they united India politically for the first time in her long history. The nationalists point out that India was not united politically: a third of the land was ruled by princes and was at least nominally independent. Besides, ask the Indians, what good would political unity have been when the root of British policy was "divide and rule," when the imperialists intentionally encouraged disunity between Hindus and Muslims and finally left the land torn into two nations, India and Pakistan? So the argument goes on and on.

What seems sure is that, for better or for worse, British rule of India was unavoidable. England *had* to find new ways to order her economic life. She could do nothing but allow her manufacturing class to come to the forefront and, given the new tools that technology placed in their hands, to reconstitute the nation as a capitalist and an industrial one. But to do so, England had to find the things she needed in order to feed her industries. There sat India, a treasure trove of those very things.

If just then India had herself been in a period of youthful growth and expansion, if she had also been bursting with powerful new life, England might not have succeeded in subduing her. But at the same time that England was pushing into the new world of modern technology, India was resting content with herself. In her rigid isolation, India, like a magnificent but hollow doll, was easily blown over by the mighty wind of new industrial needs in Europe. So much more backward than India at first, England leap-frogged into the future.

Indians could hardly help becoming angry at being always the bottom men in so serious a game. Yet the beginnings of the movement to oust the British were incredibly benign. The great organization of the independence fight, the Indian National Congress, was formed shortly before the beginning of the twentieth century by an Englishman! His purpose was to create a forum wherein educated Indians could voice their criticisms of the British government, lest their dissatisfactions take more threatening forms. It was assumed that their voices would be soft, gentle, controlled. And they were . . . at first.

But after thirty years of more or less polite resolutions, a great change happened upon the Congress. That change took the unimposing form of a tiny man, wrinkled, clad in homespun, soft-voiced, saintlike, and a proven politician of the highest order. Mohandas Gandhi had shortly before returned from South Africa. He had journeyed to that distant land as a young lawyer to argue the case of an Indian businessman living there. Never very successful in his profession at home, he stayed in South Africa to ferment and mold demands for kinder treatment of Indians, badly discriminated against in their adopted land. In the process he forged a new technique, called *satyagraha*, or nonviolent resistance.

Although he had been far away for twenty years, when Gandhi returned to India he was more widely known, probably, than he would have been had he stayed in the land of his birth. The fight of the South African Indians had fired spirits at home, and Gandhi almost immediately assumed a role of leadership in the infant struggle for self-determination.

Soon after his arrival, he launched the first major nation-wide campaign of the Congress. Everywhere people implemented the new method and offered nonviolent resistance to the British rulers.

Gandhi believed that one's enemies should never be despised. He did not want to wring concessions from them. He sought instead to convince them through his actions that his cause was just, so that they might grant him his wish willingly. In fact, though, Gandhi had the knack of the born politician to gauge the desires of his followers and to give voice to them in mighty uprisings by masses of people. Three times in three decades Gandhi was the wind sculpting a great swell of popular indignation, a tidal wave generated by the foreign rulers' unequal treatment of their subject people.

But each time Gandhi's movement failed to bring enlightenment to the rulers. Every nonviolent movement was met by the British with force, whether the police were armed with clubs or with guns, they used their weapons with a most unenlightened alacrity. Thousands were imprisoned, the leaders for many long years.

Like the surface of the Indian ocean during a typhoon, the swelling movement of the Indian people rose up and plunged down: up to the heights of the first surge in 1919, down to the depths of Hindu-Muslim slaughter that followed the failure of the campaign; back up again to the great Salt March by Gandhi in 1931, and again sharply down to communal slaughter before the rulers allowed a drop more Indian participation in government affairs. The next sharp rise came in 1942 when the Quit India movement began, the only one that was largely leaderless. Gandhi and the other important Congress figures had been jailed at first rumor of a coming fight, for these were war years when the British were very touchy indeed.

The Quit India movement was probably the most intimidating to the British. For the first time the demand was made for complete withdrawal of the British; that withdrawal was made a precondition for Indian cooperation in the war effort. Only as a free nation, said the nationalists, can we take our place in the ranks of nations fighting to free subject peoples. If we are made to fight while still subjects ourselves, then we can see no vital difference between so-called democracy in Britain and fascism in Germany, and we shall remain neutral.

More threatening, though, than the demand was the form of the movement. Millions of plain folk, the raw stuff of which the British had always thought its support in war-time would come, rebelled. Moreover, the upsurge proved that the Congress leaders had not themselves created the independence movement. Instead it began to appear that they had moderated it, had kept it polite and nonviolent. For in their absence, the 1942 movement broke out all over the country without any central coordination. Telegraph lines were cut, bridges destroyed, police stations captured. Gandhi had before always imposed a strict rule against destructiveness and had, in fact, point-blank cancelled the first movement when some policemen in a tiny forgotten village were killed.

The Quit India movement was a true rebellion. But like its grandfather a hundred years before, it flared only briefly before dying out. Nonetheless, like its ancestor, it left the government with a stubborn "What-if?" hanging over its head. Full well did the rulers know that they would have been rulers no more had the uprising not died a natural death.

By the time World War II had ended, it was clear that British rule in India was drawing to an end. In the mouths of the nationalists was a bitter taste from the stubborn refusal of the English to include Indians in their grand ideas about self-determination, a self-determination, it seemed, for "Europeans only." Surrounding the souls of Indians, moreover, was an ache of horror at the dreadful famine in Bengal, caused by government requisitioning of food supplies for troops and the indifference of the administration to the wretchedness of the millions who consequently starved to death in that "rice-basket" province. Nationalism in the colony had never been more determined.

No less formidable was the exhaustion of the "mother-land." The British had won the war. Yet they had been beaten. When the British had conquered India two centuries before, they had been a young and vital nation overcoming an exhausted one. Now the position was reversed. The power of forces demanding independence surged in India's veins, while England lay panting, anemic and worn. If the British had any remaining hopes of holding their prize, a naval rebellion in Bombay in 1946 stilled them forever.

The details of the transfer began to be worked out. Ghandi had previously towered over all the many leaders of the nationalist movement. But now as independence drew near, two others moved to the fore and stayed there.

The first was Jawaharlal Nehru. From his early manhood, Nehru's life had been the independence movement. As president of the Congress for many terms; as friend to Ghandi, who made it clear that Jawaharlal was to be his successor; as brilliant historian and moving public speaker, Nehru had established for himself a central role in the movement. Now he was the logical choice to be the new nation's first prime minister. As PM-designate he played the central role in negotiating the transfer of power.

So closely is Nehru identified with India that an Indian traveling in distant lands is often greeted with the exclamation: "Ah, India! Nehru!" Yet Nehru himself was less an Indian than most of his coleaders. Educated in England, son of a wealthy family, inspired by the great thinkers of Europe, Karl Marx among them, Nehru often seemed far more a westerner than a child of his homeland. His reflections in his autobiography, *Toward Freedom*, and in his masterful history, *The Discovery of India*, are foreign to the thinking of the country. Yet when Nehru as a budding agitator first visited the villages of his native province, he found an identity with his peasant audience so immediate and so powerful that his words moved them as few others' could. Nehru himself remarked of the paradox. He said that he stood between two worlds, that he was neither wholly of India nor wholly of the West.

To an extent Nehru resolved the dilemma by declaring himself to be a universal man.

What is my inheritance? To what am I heir? To all that humanity has achieved during tens of thousands of years, to all that it has thought and felt and suffered and taken pleasure in, to its cries of triumph and its bitter agony of defeat, to that astonishing adventure of man which began so long ago and yet continues and beckons us. To all this and more, in common with all men.*

Nehru, like Asoka before him, was a philosopher-statesman. Until his country became independent, he was rather more philosopher than statesman, although his abilities as an administrator and a politician were considerable. After independence he became very much more the statesman, the practical man of affairs. His resemblance to Asoka diminished. He recognized always the needs of the moment. Whatever his personal theories and his own heart's desires for his people, he sagely bowed to the inevitable. In the process he kept his power to the end—and he failed to realize his dream of a

* Jawaharlal Nehru, *op. cit.*, page 37.

renewed, modernized, vigorous, dignified India.

Nehru's partner in importance during the days just before independence was a man whose name is little known to the world today: Mohammad Ali Jinnah. Nehru sought to speak for humanity. Jinnah forced him to become the voice of Hindu India. For Jinnah was the champion of the Muslims in India. A little more than a year before India became a nation, Jinnah first insisted that Muslims should have their own nation, to be called Pakistan. The Congress leaders, from Gandhi and Nehru through unknown officials in the villages, were shocked, dismayed and incredulous at the idea. Both Nehru and Gandhi had always insisted that India must be the home of all peoples, all creeds, all religions. The president of the Congress at that time was a Muslim. Nehru ridiculed the idea that Muslims were a different nation. He thought incredible the idea that they might ever form an independent state in the subcontinent.

Yet that is what they did only a few months later. When India became independent, a second state, Pakistan, was carved out of her northwestern provinces and from the eastern portion of Bengal. Pakistan was Jinnah's creation, a brainchild that displaced millions from their homes, led to massacres on a scale rarely seen in history, and unsettled the futures of five hundred million people. Today, Pakistan has been torn asunder by furious hatreds and civil warfare.

Jinnah was as much the creation of Hindu-Muslim hatreds as he was their creator. Early in the independence movement, Jinnah had been a prominent Congress member. A supporter of Gandhi, he played a major role in the first national movement, which Gandhi purposely built around an issue dear to the hearts of Muslims in India. Yet time after time, as the political movement died in failure, religious hatreds flared up and claimed their victims.

In a sense, both Jinnah and the hope of a healthy, modern India were among those victims. Jinnah was a thoroughly westernized Bombay lawyer. Tall, thin, fastidiously dressed, cold and sharp of mind, he was steadily embittered by the strife. The blame, he felt, lay with the Hindus, who failed to appreciate his people's differences and worth. The idea of Pakistan may have grown in his mind over many decades. But only in the chaotic, hate-filled days just before independence dared he voice the demand seriously.

Many have claimed that the British granted nationhood to Pakistan in order to drive a lasting wedge into the subcontinent of India, a wedge that would allow them to maintain some measure of control. In fact, Pakistan has been everybody's wedge. Friendly with everybody, receiving arms and aid at one time or another from the U.S.A. and China, from Britain and the U.S.S.R., Pakistan has continually been engaged in conflict with India. The Indians likewise have often seemed to frame their national policy with the sole idea of smiting the Pakistanis. The conflict has helped to keep both nations from growing and progressing as they might have done.

Pakistan is not, however, by any means India's major problem. That dubious honor goes instead to her own internal complexity. In other lands, in England or France or Russia, one class or another has grasped its own future in its two hands and propelled its nation into new ages.

In India, though, no class or group has done likewise, for none is dynamic enough, none sure enough of its own importance, to do so. Factory workers are peasants come to town. They toil like proletarians and think like farmers. The industrialists are maharajas gone modern, but visualizing themselves as the fathers of their former subjects. The politicians are democrats jealously guarding the privileges that allow them to live like maharajas.

In form India is a modern state. She has a modern capital, New Delhi, where sits a modern Parliament. She has an indirectly elected president whose job is mostly ceremonial, and an indirectly elected prime minister whose job is to administer the state. She has dozens of universities and research institutes where projects of the highest technical caliber are going on. She has scientists as imaginative and well-trained as any in America or Russia. She has the world's highest dam, steel mills that look like they've just arrived from Pittsburgh, cities designed by geniuses like Corbusier.

In fact, though, India is not a modern nation. She is a living museum. New forms come but old ones do not die; they coexist. Carpenters in million-dollar factories use hammers to drive screws. The world's highest dam was built by sari-clad peasant women carrying baskets of cement on their heads up bamboo scaffolds. Farmers with up-to-date mechanized wheat farms in Punjab enjoy Sunday rice grown by the peasants of another province in fields tilled by buffalos and wooden plows. The woman prime minister addresses audiences studded with the black robes of women in *purdah*. Ancient junks glide through Bombay harbor past the domes of an atomic reactor.

India's history, long and complex, is written in the present tense.

16

The Feel of the Land: A Journey Through India

THUS DO the bullock cart and the motorbike carry people in India along the routes of their varying lives. Now we know something about a few of those people—Seema and Gopal, Tinku and Gita and Yogendra Chandra. We have glimpsed the road they travel.

But any country is more than the sum of her people and their customs. Most especially is this true of India. India is also her sounds and her smells, her swift winds and her clammy heat; the grace with which her women move as they carry water jugs atop their heads; the jangle of glass bangles; the regal humps of bullocks, and the pained squeak of bullock carts; a thousand flowers and a thousand fruits; a group of austerely white-clad women clanging bells and chanting as they march in procession toward a temple; the delicate, voluptuously posed figures carved on the tower of a Hindu temple; the round dome of a Muslim mosque covered with blue and green glazed tiles; the calls of hawkers, and the quibbling of shoppers; the long, face-obscuring, flowing costumes of some women, and the short, bare-chested sarongs of others.

Quick glimpses of a land, telling you nothing beyond that your eyes can see, your nostrils sniff, your ears hear, permit you to sense only the surface of the place. Critics of city-a-day tours say that is not enough. True, it is not. Yet once you know something of the life of India, then the sights, the sounds, the smells add an enchantment and a depth, a will to experience the country firsthand as no simple meeting with this or that individual can do.

Let us now travel through the land.

In Delhi we first met Seema. In Delhi our itinerary begins. City of two eras, Delhi is the hub of modern India as it was of Moghul India. The old and the new cities have a border between them but they are not divided. Modern homes can be found in Old Delhi. Ancient forts and tombs spot New Delhi. Memorials to the fathers of the modern nation, Nehru and Gandhi, lie on the river bank in Old Delhi, opposite the imposing walls of the Moghul's Red Fort.

The road dividing the memorials from the fort is Ring Road, a divided highway that encircles Delhi, the same road on which the motorcyclist of Chapter One entered the city. Raj Ghat, the Gandhi memorial built on the riverside spot where the leader was cremated, is usually the first stop on a sightseeing tour of Old Delhi. It is a beautifully landscaped park, simple, yet an eloquent memorial to the man it honors. No monument or gaudy tower marks his memory. There is nothing here but nature and a simple concrete path leading to the spot of the cremation. That very simplicity, coupled with the crowds of quiet visitors who always throng here, gives the park its dignity. Just so did his simplicity and the love with which he was regarded mark Gandhi as a Mahatma, a great man.

But if the Gandhi memorial shouts simplicity, Red Fort

opposite does no such thing. High walls rise from a green field. Once, the River Jamuna flowed against those walls. But the course of the river has changed, and now boys fly kites and washermen lay long white *dhotis* to dry where the water used to run. This is the back side of Red Fort. To reach the front requires a ride of no little distance along the red wall. Peaked Moghul arches greet the visitor. Within, shops line an outer courtyard. Souvenirs made of straw and ivory are offered where the queens of the emperors in centuries past probably fingered elegant brocades and intricate gold-filigree baubles.

The inner courtyard is today a military encampment. Along the back of the fort are the original buildings of the emperors: walls of latticed stone, marble that hints of the gems once inlaid there but now gone, long channels where the baths of the queens ran cool and clean.

Far away across Delhi, deep in the new city built by the British, is the center of today's government. Its heart is a majestic avenue, Rajpath, Road of the State. It is lined with green meadows through which run waterways inspired by the baths of the Moghuls. At its foot is India Gate, a stone arch memorial to the soldiers of the Indian Army killed in the First World War. Just behind it across a busy traffic circle is a curious monument. A concrete umbrella shades an empty pedestal. Here once sat a statue of King George V. Many years after independence the statue was removed, not without heated debate first. Still the arguments continue over whose image should replace that of the unseated King-Emperor. Nothing could better symbolize India today then does that vacant throne. At the other end of Rajpath is Rashtrapati Bhavan, the president's mansion. It was built to house the British Viceroy, who ruled India in the King's name. When the last Viceroy handed over power to Prime Minister Nehru,

Gandhi suggested that the mansion be made a hospital for the poor. But the new rulers decided that pomp was, after all, a useful tool in the hands of democratic leaders, and so Rashtrapati Bhavan remains the seat of the mighty. It is a large building topped with domes. Ordinarily a bit ludicrous, the mansion becomes truly magnificent twice a year. For Diwali its eaves, domes and stairs are lined with tiny electric lights, and thousands come to admire the beauty of the scene. Soon afterward the gardens bloom with winter flowers, a sense-tingling profusion of color and perfume, which seems to apologize for the austerity of the building to which the exotic plants owe their existence.

From Delhi most visitors travel to Agra, a city about four hours' drive to the south. Capital of some of the Moghul emperors, Agra houses the most famous building of all India: the Taj Mahal. But long before he spots the white towers of the Taj, the traveler by car is treated to a thrill as great as any he'll find during his stay in India. He meets the Indian road.

If you walk through a bazaar in India, you are sure that all the life of the land is bubbling through those narrow lanes. If you then travel somewhere by train, you feel you were mistaken, that the stations and track-sides are the arteries through which India's life-blood flows. But when you come to the roads, then you know for certain that you have found the very heart of the country.

The road runs straight and narrow. Stretching to the horizon on either side are fields, green and stubbly with new rice, or barren except for patches of yellow mustard, or rippling golden brown before the harvest, depending on the time of year. Every device known throughout the history of mankind is working actively in these fields to move water. There a camel slowly plods around a wooden water wheel. Further on two bullocks do the same endless task. But then you are jerked rudely through the centuries, for in the very next field an electric water pump is spurting water against the sky. And then again you plummet back to eons past: two men work a gouged bamboo paddle levered against a pole, rhythmically dipping it into a deep puddle of rain water, then see-sawing it up to spill the water into clay irrigation channels.

Brown-skinned, bony-ribbed farmers, their loins and their heads wrapped in gray-white cloths, dumbly follow pairs of bullocks pulling plows. Women stoop low, their saris hiked up at their waists, weeding and transplanting. Naked boys sit side-saddle on long-haired, doleful black buffalos that wander placidly, steadily, endlessly toward nowhere.

Meanwhile, life spills into the road itself. People jog-trot along to a weekly market, baskets of vegetables on their heads, leashed goats and calves straggling along behind. Children squat by the roadside; when they are not playing with pebbles or cheering the passing autos, they are peacefully defecating. Serenely dignified cattle cross the road, singly and in coveys, confidently oblivious of the beeping cars rushing toward and around them. Women spread grain to dry in the sunny middle of the highway. Ducks and chickens follow, pecking at what has been carefully laid out to be preserved. Camels, buffalos, horses, bullocks pull a baker's variety of wooden carts, all on two wheels, large or small, all creaking and jousling.

So full are the trees and roadside with animal life that one wonders at the interest zoos arouse here. Monkeys drop from the twisted limbs of banyan trees. Small, fast-winged parrots screech through the leaves, swooping low across the road. Geese, ducks and chickens make way for regal wild peacocks. Pairs of kids, frozen by panic in the middle of the road as a car approaches, dart here and there, bleating helplessly. Elephants do the work of bulldozers where roads are being built. Hairless, white, big-bellied pigs grunt along. Trains of donkeys carry clay pots or enormous heaps of straw. Mangy dogs blink disinterestedly at well-fed cats. Vultures hungrily oversee the scene from perches high in the treetops.

A ramshackle bus lumbers down the road. Its sky-blue paint, trimmed in faded yellow and decorated with primroses, is almost obscured by the billows of gray smoke coughed forth from its rattling rear end. From the luggage rack on top, the eight legs of a pair of rope-mattressed *charpoys* stick straight up. As the bus passes, the people inside stare down at the curiosity going by: you in your hired Chevrolet.

With a regularity benumbing in its endlessness, the fields alternate with jumbled up, mud-walled villages. The houses are a chaos of form; where does one end, the next begin? But what is uncertain in the lines of the buildings is very distinct in the stacks of cow-dung patties, artistically piled up to form graceful domes.

Now and then it is not a village that breaks the fields, but a town. You turn a curve and find yourself plump in the middle of a crowded bazaar lane. Where has the highway gone? Here are piles of vegetables, sacks of rice and flour, cart-loads of fruits, all being fingered and haggled over by shoppers who grudgingly allow the beeping automobiles to trickle through their thick ranks.

Behind the bazaar are the steep walls of the houses. Every plains town in India is like every other. Flat-roofed, flat-sided, the buildings are motley piles of brick and concrete, their lines and boundaries as jumbled as those of the mud houses in the villages. But where the village buildings may form a charmingly natural group clustered around a rare grove of trees, the townhouses stand naked and ugly, huddled together behind bleak walls as if the endless space of the fields beyond threatened their very existence.

The towns are incongruous, but not altogether unexpected. They are not out of phase with the fields and villages. Totally unbelievable, though, are the smokestacks that suddenly loom above the paddy fields, belching black exhaust over the steel rafters of a factory roof. The factories that here and there dot the countryside are dramatic reminders that in India time runs in two directions at once.

No more believable are the tractors that grace some parts of the Indian scene. Like rare birds they move through the fields, more exotic than the peacocks that unfurl their grand tails for the pleasure of passing travelers.

Endlessly intriguing is the life that streams past our car windows. A washerman spreads white *dhotis* on the grass to dry while his womenfolk down at the river beat clothing against flat stones, splashing them regularly with muddy water. A turbaned graybeard squats on his *charpoy* smoking a *hookah*. A man sits on the ground, his outstretched toes holding taut the jute that his fingers deftly spin. A family waits for a bus. The father fingers the end of his *dhoti* as he peers anxiously down the road. The mother stares patiently at nothing as she squats by his side, nursing one baby and wiping the nose of another with her fingers. The older children contentedly throw clods of mud at passing cars. Past them walks a man with a jaunty spring in his gait. On his head he balances a pole from which hangs, streaming grandly out behind him, his drying laundry.

Finally we arrive in the squalid hustle of Agra, a town with a history short by Indian standards. It owes its fame to the passion for building of a few Moghul emperors. Grandest among their products is the Taj Mahal.

We walk through the peaked arch of the gateway, and immediately the gushing vitality of the road, of the town, of India herself is left behind. Before us is perfect serenity embodied in marble. Here is another India, one more akin, perhaps, to what you had expected. This love memorial to a dead queen breathes the calm majesty, the inscrutable placidity with which the spirit of the East is commonly credited. We stare at it from afar. We wander slowly through the meadow-like approaches, along the inevitable Moghul waterway. We shed our shoes to enter the shrine proper and climb the marble steps to the tomb above. We admire the carving and inlay work of its façade, and we marvel at the wealth that sank so many millions of precious gems into stone. Then we listen wondrously to the echo of the inner tomb chamber. Finally, we slowly depart.

Outside, the bustle that is everyday India again claims us, and we hurry back to Delhi to catch a northerly train. It is a night train, and we relax in the air-conditioned luxury of a well-provided Pullman car. When the train stops now and then at a station, we awake long enough to glimpse the tea and sweetmeat hawkers strolling past, to read the doleful expression in the child beggar's face, to see the huddled forms of travelers sleeping under gray rags on the platform floor. Then again the train moves on. In the morning, after a brief glimpse of lush Punjabi fields and of pert Punjabi misses bicycling smartly along the roads, we leave the train at Pathankot. From here the Himalayas rise. We can see them smoke-blue and hazily obscure to the north.

A bus takes us up. It is crowded with Indian tourists, their legs comfortably folded under them to make way for huge baskets of food, kerosene stoves, jute-covered water jugs, great-mountains of bedding, plastic pails filled with baby covers made from old saris, all the needs of families setting out determined to enjoy a holiday far from the hot plains of their everyday lives. On top of the bus is piled more luggage: cloth-wrapped suitcases, baby buggies, tin trunks, more bedding rolls. Servants traveling with these upper-middle-class families scamper happily from seat to seat, distributing cold *chapatis* and vegetable curries to their masters. People call cozy comments to each other, burrow into their bags, laugh at the antics of the children and seem to be totally oblivious to the violent lurching of the bus.

The driver is a young turbaned Sikh. He drives with all the élan of his warrior forefathers. Hairpin turns are to him a chance to display his bravado. He takes them at speeds that make the overladen bus, and us with it, shiver.

All the while the hills rise majestically ahead. Anyone not too busy to look through the smoky windows will glory in the steep cliffs terraced with paddy fields. Little waterfalls splash by the roadside. Four goats sit casually atop a narrow retaining wall. Beneath their overhanging hoofs is a drop that must surely end in the deepest pit of hell.

All day the bus speeds upward. At night the travelers stop at a meager hotel in a hamlet composed solely of hotels. At dawn caravans of buses continue the journey. By noon they reach the Valley of Kashmir: a flat oval surrounded by snow-peaks and cut through the middle by the wandering River Jhelum. At the far end of the valley is the city of Srinagar, our destination.

Srinagar is built around lakes and rivers. Water consequently molds the ways of its people, Muslims who still believe it essential to a man's dignity for him to marry at least four times. Narrow, gondola-like boats, *shikaras*, carry the Kashmiris from their huts, built on stilts lest the whimsical waters wash their flimsy walls away, to river-side stores at which customers shop without ever leaving their boats. Not bullock carts but *shikaras* carry the tillers to their vegetable gardens, planted on clods of earth floating on the lakes. The women paddle to weed patches and harvest the stuff by twirling long poles amid the plants and then deftly hauling them aboard. The weeds are fodder, vegetable, and fertilizer in one.

The women are shy. Faced with a camera, they giggle, turn away and flap their hands negatively. It's a pity, for they are among the most beautiful women in India, a land of feminine beauty. Theirs is a delicate loveliness, offset by the baggy fullness of their trousers and loose, long overjackets. Full scarves cover their heads, tied tightly around their sharp-planed foreheads, close above their huge dark eyes. In their ears they wear enormous ornaments reaching to their shoulders and often supported by chains passing over their heads.

If we had time, we might ride donkeys up into the hills to one of the high meadows, or to a glacier. But we hurry instead away from the cool Valley of Kashmir for a journey down through Delhi, and thence deep into the desert of Rajasthan to the south. Where is the shadow of those green terraced hills in this bleached sand? No tinkling waterfalls break the endless monotony of this dull horizon. No colorful flowers in perpetual bloom sweeten the uniformity of these brownish shrubs.

Yet that is not really true. For here the skirts of the Rajasthani girls wear all the color and sparkle of flowers. Vivid red, green, yellow and blue embroidery surrounds tiny mirrors, twinkling like sunlight on a mountain lake. The majesty with which two-humped camels lumber across the desert, their riders silhouetted against the pink sunset, remind us of the steeply rolling hills.

From the stuff of that sunset was built the city of Jaipur, the famed pink city of maharajas, to which we now come. As magically as the hues of the evening sky are transformed into the walls of a city, just as magically do the maharajas who once dwelt there claim us as their own as soon as we've checked into our hotel. It is a palace gone commercial. Our suite might have been a nursery in which scholars from many lands taught exotic alphabets to royal children. It might also have been a queen's boudoir, or a chambermaid's broom closet. Whatever it was, it is elegant, regal, yet modern.

Jaipur, an eighteenth-century city built by the astronomer-prince Maharaja Jai Singh, is surrounded by rugged hills. This natural fortification is seconded by a medieval wall that rings the city. The town was clearly intended to be a fortress, yet Jai Singh built with a delicacy that belies this purpose. Everywhere we turn, we find palaces. They house small, elegant, livable rooms instead of the huge formal chambers of other places. Some boast fantastic façades, like the honeycomb front of the Palace of Winds. Nearby is Jai Singh's observatory; like the rest of the city, it too is built of pink sandstone and on a grand scale.

Jaipur is a jewel carved from the raw stuff of desert Rajasthan. Udaipur, ninety minutes by air to the south, is a fantasy that denies the very existence of the great desert. The hills surrounding Udaipur are rich with natural greenery. Six hundred years ago, the prince who ruled here dreamed of a sparkling blue lake to reflect those hills, and so he built one. Two hundred years later, another raja built an island on the lake and there constructed a white dove of a palace. It floats on the deep blue waters against a background of green hills and its own white reflection. Today it is the Lake Palace Hotel.

All around Udaipur are lakes and palaces built by the Rajputs of the region. In ancient times, it is said, the Rajasthani desert was irrigated and bloomed with vegetation. The Rajputs renewed that irrigation system, using their lakes as a source of water. Parts of the network of waterways are operative today.

(Our next stop, Bombay, is the most thoroughly modern of India's four big metropolises. A chain of mountains bordering the coast, the Western Ghats, is its garden. The Arabian Ocean is its front yard. The city is built on a chain of seven islands. Marine Drive, a wealthy residential street, curves around a deep bay. To the east across a narrow strip of land is the impressive arch of the Gateway of India. It overlooks a busy harbor where the tall sails of fishing junks glide past low sleek tankers unloading oil for Trombay, site of a nuclear reactor.

The citizens of Bombay are a cosmopolitan blending of peoples. A five-year-old living in Bombay is apt to speak Gujarati, Marathi, Hindi, English and possibly Persian as well. The streets, shaded by modern multi-storied buildings in the center of town, are busy with pavement-dwellers. Clouds of beggars dog the steps of strollers along Marine Drive. These women pull their saris through their legs to form buttocks-hugging pantaloons. They carry sleepy infants and stick like leeches to their prey.

If their victims are not foreigners, they are usually young men with fastidiously shaped sideburns and bell-bottom dacron and cotton trousers. On their arms hang bobbed-hair girls wearing *churidars*, which fit their legs like tights, and *kurtas* with flowing sleeves and A-shaped lines. Prosperous middle-aged family men stroll too, with their well-dressed children and wives. These matrons wear their saris with the trains draped from back to front over the right shoulder, exactly the opposite of the style worn elsewhere.

Visitors are apt to think of Bombay as a huge extension of modern Marine Drive. But actually Bombay is miles of battered lower middle-class tenements, broken occasionally by brand new skyscrapers bearing the signboards of Tata and Cadbury Chocolate and Colgate-India. It is even more miles of stinking shanty towns, clustered around stagnant pools of oil-covered water. It is hundreds of cotton mills and dozens of teeming docks.

It is also the famous Crawford Market, a maze of tiny shops, an endless bazaar that seems to be all entrance, no exit. Cottons and silks and satins crowd together in open-fronted booths along rows of aisles. Electrical appliances shipped from Japan and the West and smuggled past Indian customs inspectors are sold openly in other rows. Plastic bowls and straw mats and hot-water heaters and gold-embroidered saris and raw-silk evening jackets are offered to passing tourists by eager-eyed would-be guides. They run at the heels of likely customers chanting: "*Memsahib* want silk? *Memsahib* want electric iron? I know ver-r-r-ry good shop. I show way."

India is too vast, too varied, too rich to be toured with anything but a nagging sense of omission. We now fly far south, stopping too briefly in Aurangabad to visit the Ellora and Ajanta caves, too briefly in Hyderabad, too briefly in Bangalore, garden city of planned suburbs and enormous factories.

We cannot leave India, though, without seeing one of the many wildlife parks, and so we pause now at Mudumalai Game Sanctuary in the lush Nilgiri Hills. Our guide perches monkey-like near the neck of the elephant that transports us through the forest. He points out tigers, bears, deer, rhinos, panthers. Monkeys cavort in the branches overhead; birds fly from tree to tree.

Now we return to city life, and the city is one of the most complex in the world: Cochin, main port of the Malabar Coast in Kerala. Here we visit a variety of temples and churches and synagogues. We cross the straits to Vypeen Island, its name a relic of Dutch settlers, its beaches a base for Chinese fishing nets. Canals wind past houses built on stilts. The harbor looks like a still lagoon, yet it hums with activity, handling more than a million and a half tons of cargo every year.

From Cochin we travel east through the tropical magnificence of Kerala into the state of Tamilnadu, to the town of Madurai. Madurai is a living museum of south Indian Hindu architecture. Its hub, the Meenakshi Temple, is an ancient place that has grown and been used and loved through the centuries. Its nine gateways are carved with brightly painted effigies of thousands of gods and goddesses, although the temple itself is a shrine to Shiva and his wife Meenakshi. Inside, casual Hindu worship goes on endlessly. Slim, small-boned south Indian women, their dark hair parted in two unbound plaits, shop at rows of noisy stalls for flowers and *prasad*, fruits and sweets, to offer to the goddess. Pilgrims bathe in the courtyard. Guides raucously offer their services in a dozen tongues. Formidable though the noise and activity is, it does not distract us from our wonder in the Hall of a Thousand Pillars, where, it is rumored, you can find something new no matter how often you return. For each of the pillars is carved with figures; somewhere in that enormous hall you can find the expression of any human mood and state imaginable.

Our next flying stop is Madras, a city that sprawls over fifty square miles, yet reminds one more of a drowsy market town than of a great metropolis. Miles of beaches along the Bay of Bengal coast add to the appearance of leisure. Don't try to swim here, though. These are shark-infested waters. Madras is the center of resistance to the use of Hindi as the national language. But strolling through the streets, we find it incredible that these slight-framed, dark-complexioned, energetic, pleasant-featured men and gracefully self-confident women are capable of the violence and passion that has held the language policy of the country at bay for so many years. There are few tourist spots here, but if you love dance you will be glad to have included Madras in your itinerary. Bharat Natyam, a classical dance-drama form, is enjoying a revival in the city; nowhere else can you see it performed so expertly.

In Madras we leave the south and fly northeast, far away to Calcutta. Many a visitor who has returned home to shudder over horrible memories of India saw Calcutta and no place else. Anybody who has stopped, however briefly, in this the largest city of India, can tell a good number of hair-raising stories. Calcutta is the City of Revolution, the City of Chaos, the City from which the Black Hole has never been entirely erased. Calcutta should be off-limits to tourists who stop only long enough to witness its poverty.

The sticky heat of Bengal rises from Calcutta's pavements in distorting waves. Across Chowringhee, the main shopping street, the once placid Maidan, or central park, has been invaded by a tram depot. Rapid-fire trams clatter into the park; a pedestrian wanting to cross the tracks jumps back from near catastrophe a dozen times before he succeeds in leaping to the other side. The loose-limbed wearers of flowing *dhotis* and long-tailed shirts called *jama* lope along the streets—not the sidewalks, which are the preserve of tourists, hawkers and cows. The latter, of course, are not confined to the footways; they stray blandly through the rushing traffic, which aims for their swishing tails in the hope the beasts will continue moving in the same direction. Rickshaw-pullers trot along the gutters through muck and dung, their human cargo elevated to another, more sanitary world. Policemen yawn into large white handkerchiefs, while hawkers squat beside them in the road, selling fruits and vegetables to leisurely quibbling customers. Policemen, vendors and shoppers all behave as if the honking of the cars stopped dead by this commerce were the sweet tittering of nightingales.

If the cities of India were automobiles, New Delhi would be

a chauffer-driven Volkswagen, Bombay a rushing Fiat, Calcutta a Rolls-Royce stalled in deep mud.

At dusk the cooking buckets are hauled to the pavements, and cow-dung fires are lighted. So thick is the smoke that the city seems to be burning, an appearance not far from the fact. A visiting stroller through the maze of alleys is a source of wonderment to the population. From tiny, low-ceilinged rooms, visible through the cracks in small, shuttered windows, people pour out to watch. Naked infants peek from behind the bedraggled saris of hot, weary mothers, permanent lines of fatigue etched over their noses. Dressed in wash-grayed undershirts and faded *lungis,* the ankle-length, saronglike skirts equally popular among the ordinary males of Bengal and the elegant females of Delhi and Bombay, men squat against the walls and stare. Cattle look up; goats bleat fearfully; chickens and ducks cackle.

Here and there among the slum pavements are decayed mansions. At first glance they appear to be abrupt intruders into the huddled jungle of concrete shanties. But a closer look reveals that they have long since been overtaken by the tropical growth of the slum. Grecian statues on lawns and roofs stare blankly at the passerby. From once-fashionable columns hang laundry. Dirt tries to obscure brilliant mosaic floors, but doesn't quite succeed. Gloom and damp-rot inhabit these senile houses; cobwebs clothe their carved cornices; bats glide through their high-ceilinged salons. Ghostly they are, but far from deserted. Through dusky hallways rings the laughter of many children playing. From formal verandas rises the smoke of cow-dung fires. In ornate fountains women shampoo their hair, and men bathe their underarms. Every inch of dilapidated majesty rings with the business of living.

Visitors to Calcutta weep for its poverty. Residents shout their pride in its vitality. Bengalis live the public life as few people do. Political parties, agitations, and demonstrations are as numerous as street-dwellers. Londoners are solemn; New Yorkers harried. But Calcuttans fill their streets with laughter and song. A gay religious parade marches down one side of a busy, traffic-tied street, while angry, slogan-shouting, red-flag-waving strikers march up the other. Calcutta is a cultured city. It's citizens love Rabindranath Tagore, swell proudly at the mention of his dance-drama, display his paintings and image everywhere. Every school boy sings the poetry of Rabindranath. But the very same people also throw their garbage to the crows, whose racket drowns all conversation at dusk. Calcuttans blithely tie their motor traffic into knots, crudely berate their neighbors for drawing more than their share of scarce water during the four hours daily the taps give forth . . . and hang garlands on portraits of the Poet.

On our journey through India, from Delhi north to the hills, south to Madras, we may have formed some theories about the land, some estimates of its people. Calcutta blows them away, and we leave for home confused, warmed, appalled, angry, sad, chuckling over memories of friendliness and hospitality, terrified, delighted, happy we came and so thoroughly shaken that the world will never again be quite so neatly round as it once was.

Bibliography

Anand, Mulk Raj, *Indian Fairy Tales*, Kutub–Popular, Bombay, 1946

Chaudhuri, Nirad C., *The Autobiography of an Unknown Indian*, Macmillan, New York (also University of California Press Paperback, 1968)

Fischer, Lewis, *The Life of Mahatma Gandhi*, Harper, New York, 1950

Kosambi, Damodar Dharmanand, *Ancient India*, Monthly Review Press, New York, 1966

Naipaul, V. S., *An Area of Darkness*, Macmillan, 1965

Nair, Kusum, *Blossoms in the Dust*, New York, Praeger, 1962

Nehru, Jawaharlal, *The Discovery of India*, Asia Publishing House, 1961

———, *Toward Freedom*, Beacon Press, Boston, 1958

Panikkar, Kavalam Madhava, *The Foundations of New India*, Allen and Unwin, London, 1963

———, *A Survey of Indian History*, Asia Publishing House, 1966

Rajagopalachari, C., *Ramayana*, Bharatiya Vidya Bhawan, Bombay, [n.d.]

Spencer, Cornelia, *Made in India: The Story of India's People*, Alfred Knopf, New York, 1953

Tagore, Rabindranath, *Collected Poems and Plays*, Macmillan, New York, 1937

———, *Stories from the Panchatantra*, Children's Book Trust, New Delhi, [n.d.]

Index